LANGUAGE AND LITERACY SERIES

Dorothy S. Strickland, FOUNDING EDITOR

Celia Genishi and Donna E. Alvermann, SERIES EDITORS

ADVISORY BOARD: Richard Allington, Kathryn Au, Bernice Cullinan, Col~~~~~~~~~~~
Carole Edelsky, Shirley Brice Heath, Connie Juel, Susan Ly~~~~~~~~

For volumes in the NCRLL Collection (edited by JoBeth Allen and Donna E. Alvermann) and the Practitioners Bookshelf Series (edited by Celia Genishi and Donna E. Alvermann), as well as a complete list of titles in this series, please visit www.tcpress.com.

Critical Media Pedagogy

Teaching for Achievement in City Schools

Ernest Morrell,
Rudy Dueñas, Veronica Garcia,
and Jorge López

Teachers College, Columbia University
New York and London

Published by Teachers College Press, 1234 Amsterdam Avenue, New York, NY 10027

Library of Congress Cataloging-in-Publication Data

Morrell, Ernest, 1971–
    Critical media pedagogy : teaching for achievement in city schools / Ernest Morrell, Rudy Dueñas, Veronica Garcia, and Jorge López.
        pages cm.
    ISBN 978-0-8077-5438-2 (pbk. : alk. paper)—ISBN 978-0-8077-5439-9 (hardcover : alk. paper)
    1. Education, Urban—United States.   2. Critical pedagogy—United States.   3. Mass media and youth—United States.   4. Mass media and education—United States.   5. Mass media—Study and teaching—United States.   I. Title.
LC5141.M67 2013
370.9173′2—dc23   2012051067

ISBN 978-0-8077-5438-2 (paper)
ISBN 978-0-8077-5439-9 (hardcover)

Printed on acid-free paper
Manufactured in the United States of America

20 19 18 17 16 15 14 13   8 7 6 5 4 3 2 1

Contents

 # Introduction

It is 11:15 on a summer evening and a handful of us are in a large lecture hall in the UCLA Law School. We are in the final week of preparations for our Council of Youth Research. Lizzie, a 19-year-old alumna of our program, sits weary-eyed in the back row, her oversized headphones on her head. Next to her is seated Brian, a 16-year-old incoming senior from a nearby neighborhood in the same city. They are working on the final edits of their digital video, which will be screened to an audience of 200 people at Los Angeles City Hall before being posted on YouTube, Facebook, and our institute's website. Lizzie, a veteran director of more than 30 films, is lecturing young Brian on the importance of selecting overlays for the documentary. Brian sits and sorts through the dozens of photographs that he and his team members have taken over the past few weeks while waiting for Lizzie's approval. At 19, she is entering her sophomore year at a local college. She began working in our youth council as a sophomore in high school and, during that 4-year stretch, has made some of the most amazing short digital videos that any of us have ever seen. I look over at Lizzie and ask her if the video is going to be completed in time. "Oh yes," she assures me, "just not as good as I would like it to be." The video is indeed finished and is screened to a packed audience at Los Angeles City Hall to great acclaim. However, the group of five high school students is not satisfied. They keep promising a "director's cut." I say fine, but we still load their final piece onto our website, and in my mind, the film is done. About 2 weeks after the youth council's summer program, I am bombarded with posts from friends and colleagues around the country about this amazing video they are seeing on Facebook. Sure enough, I am "tagged" in a video from the summer seminar of 2010, a 10-minute version of the video I saw Lizzie and Brian working on just a few weeks prior. On their own time, these five high school students and their college mentor have been working on a project that they viewed as unfinished, without any encouragement or externally imposed incentives other than "getting it right," the way they wanted it. Of course, the 10-minute version of this video is phenomenal. About a week later, I received an email from one of my doctoral students from UCLA. She is one of the people who have been sending the youths' videos to

*friends and colleagues via Facebook (I have done this myself). She received a re-
sponse from an educational consultant in New York City that she shared with
me. This colleague was working with a network of city principals and used the
youth videos to focus these leaders (who collectively work with nearly 250,000
students) on directing their resources towards under-resourced schools.*

—Ernest Morrell

CITY YOUTH AND THE NEW MEDIA AGE

The lives of city youth are saturated with media—from television and
tablets, to social networks, mobile devices, and video game consoles.
Today's youth spend the majority of their waking lives as consumers
and producers of media. This interaction has both positive and potentially harmful effects. On the one hand, as the opening example
demonstrates, youth are acquiring sophisticated media production
and distribution skills that could be useful to transition to academic
achievement, professional employment, and civic engagement in the
21st century (Gee, 2003; Hill, 2009; Hobbs, 2007; Kress, 2003; Morrell,
2008). Secondary-school-aged students regularly shoot, edit, produce,
and distribute high-quality digital videos through personal websites and other social media networks such as Facebook, Twitter, and
YouTube to audiences throughout the world. Youth today blog, pin,
post, comment, and share links with social networks on a scale that, a
generation ago, would have been possible only for professional media
personnel. Youth participation in media production gives them leverage and voice on a historically unprecedented scale. This media production also facilitates the development of more literate and thoughtful
participants in our democratic process.

However, major corporations, which want to develop loyal consumers and therefore play into the insecurities of young people, also
heavily influence the media that youth consume. Corporate media are
also prone to send negative messages and reinforce stereotypes and
dominant value systems that could have deleterious effects on uncritical consumers. In *Kinderculture: The Corporate Construction of Childhood,*
Steinberg and Kincheloe (2004) argue that media encourage a culture
of consumption that places status more on what one has than what one
does. Among their charges are that corporate-controlled media promote fast foods and other products that lead to obesity and childhood

diseases; they also sell toys and games that promote violence. Even further, these media often portray negative images of city youth that influence the beliefs of the larger public, who then enact or call for hateful and harmful policies against these youth (Giroux, 1996). In each of our classrooms, students have critiqued the media and their presentation of city youth as deviants and threats to society. Even though violent crimes among youth are down over the past decade, news media will focus on youth flash mobs in London or Philadelphia more than they pay attention to the structures created by adults that lead to such rebellions.

Our goal in this book is neither to praise nor condemn the new media age, but to proclaim its existence and its significant impact on the lives of the youth that we teach. The power of new media in the lives of young people cannot be denied, and therefore, we advocate that media education be more effectively implemented into the K–12 curriculum in the United States. More specifically, we are advocating for a *critical media education.* By *critical media* we are calling for an educational process that makes young people aware of the role that media play, both positively and problematically, in shaping social thought (Kellner & Share, 2007). As educators, we want the youth we teach to understand how knowledge transmitted via the media can reinforce stereotypes and encourage people to feel badly about themselves and others. To do this, students need to be able to bring their critical reasoning skills to the decoding and analysis of texts produced across many genres—including, but not limited to, television, film, music, the Internet, print media, magazines, murals, posters, t-shirts, billboards, social networking sites, and mobile media apps. A critical media perspective also enlightens students to the potential that they have, as media producers, to shape the world they live in and to help to turn it into the world they imagine. Youth attending secondary schools in the United States need to be made more explicitly aware of their relationships with the media, and they need an education that imparts the skills they need to powerfully consume and produce new media. We are calling this process a *critical media pedagogy,* which will foster academic literacy development, academic achievement, and civic engagement in city schools. Other nations have called for media education, but their versions of media education have focused largely on the consumption of media texts. In other words, like early generations of cultural studies, most media education focuses on analyzing and deconstructing new media genres such as film, television, and print media using critical literary lenses such as feminism, Marxism, and postcolonialism.

While it is certainly important to help youth become more knowledgeable and critical consumers of corporate media, we also recognize in this historical moment the democratizing nature of media as sites of mass cultural production. In the age of text messaging, social networking, and digital video filmmaking, youth are as likely to produce via new media as they are to consume, and therefore, a critical media education in K–12 schools has to facilitate critical youth media production. And while the first generation of media education has theoretically acknowledged youth as media producers, it has not necessarily advocated a *critical stance* toward media production, nor has it looked at the considerations for historically underserved youth and their relationships toward media, past and present. Toward these ends, this book theorizes critical media production among city youth as a strategy for increasing literacy development, academic achievement, and civic engagement. Drawing from a combination of cultural studies, critical theory, sociocultural theories of learning and literacy, and empirical research on media pedagogy with city youth across two high schools and a university-based college access program for teens, we explore the applications of critical media pedagogy across English and social studies classrooms, after-school clubs, and youth organizations, noting how everyday educators and cultural workers incorporate new media into their teaching and documenting the impacts of the new media on students' learning, achievement, and engagement. With its movement of theory to practice, we envision this book as a call to action, as well as an example of critical media pedagogy and school-based media action research on and in solidarity with youth.

MEDIA CULTURAL STUDIES, CRITICAL PEDAGOGY, AND URBAN EDUCATION

Our goals with this book are both conceptual and pedagogical. Conceptually, we hope to integrate the field of cultural studies to include the voices of youth media producers, city classroom educators, and others in the field of education who work with youth in out-of-school learning environments. If cultural studies are to make the transition from a field that studies consumption to one that also theorizes counter-cultural production, it will have to more systematically and emphatically take up the question of pedagogy (Kellner, 1995; Kellner & Share, 2007;

Morrell, 2008). Therefore, one way that this work pushes on media and cultural studies is that it expands the community of scholarship to include classroom teachers and the youth themselves, who are conducting parallel research in the examples shown in this book. When youth use media tools to investigate media production to inform their own counter-media production, now that's something. Working within the frame of the book and speaking to dominant discourses, it is possible to argue that this process fosters literate production and civic engagement at once. That is, as youth become critical media producers, they also become different kinds of intellectuals and different kinds of citizens. It is also possible to argue that they become different types of artists with the potential to re-shape our cultural aesthetic while critically engaging social thought.

THEORIES OF LITERACY AND CIVIC ENGAGEMENT

Critical literacy educators view teaching as a political act (Apple, 1990). As youth who have been historically marginalized learn to read and write, a critical approach to literacy education helps them to re-read and ultimately re-write the world. Literacy, then, becomes more than an act of decoding; it becomes praxis as newly literate populations become more skilled in their ability to act powerfully upon the world (Freire, 1970; Perry, 2003). This approach to literacy is consistent with the African American tradition that has argued for freedom for literacy and literacy for freedom (Douglass, 1845; Perry, 2003). As educators who work in some of the most underperforming schools located inside of concentrations of great poverty, we envision our civic duty as linking literacy education and media production with civic participation. To do this, we draw upon political philosophers such as Locke and Rousseau and educational philosophers such as John Dewey (1900, 1902, 1916) and Paulo Freire (1970, 1998), who speak to the connection between critical education and participatory democracy. The multicultural, multimodal society of the 21st century, we argue, requires high levels of literacy for those who want to be civically engaged (Alvermann, 2001). Students who desire social justice must be critical consumers and producers of texts across multiple genres of both traditional and new media. As educators, we remain committed to the development of traditional academic literacies (Morrell, 2004; Gutierrez, 2008) and civic sensibilities, and we develop and explore in-school and non-school interventions that seek to develop both new media and traditional academic literacies. Through the examples offered in this book, we will endeavor to show how students are not just learning new media technologies, but also how they are developing confidence and academic abilities as they navigate the lessons put forward in this volume.

CRITICAL MEDIA PEDAGOGY AS A RESPONSE TO YOUTH IN CRISIS

It seems impossible these days to turn on the television or pick up a newspaper without hearing about the crisis of today's "city" youth. Whether we are talking about flash mobs, school violence, gang activity, drug use, the legal troubles of hip hop artists and athletes, or poor academic performance in failing schools, the news and the people who watch it are positioning an entire generation as a problem. While, as educators, we do not deny the presence of many troubling data that speak to the challenges our youth face, our questions are more essential and pragmatic. First of all, who *put* these youth in crisis? What is it that we, the "older" population, have done to precipitate this crisis? And second, what can be done to end it?

As authors, our belief is that young people have not, as a collective entity, put themselves in crisis. They are facing the problems they do largely because of what adults have done or, more accurately, what we have not done. Although our aim is to write a book about youth media production inside of schools, our larger goal is to theorize pedagogies of youth empowerment that benefit them socially as well as academically—precisely because of the challenges that society has created for them. No matter what the micro-questions are that surround today's youth, the answers begin with adults who often overlook the potential of young people. The answer begins with our attempt to understand the lives of youth and to incorporate this understanding into lessons that reach youth on an existential as well as intellectual level. Although this is a book that will celebrate many amazing things that young people have done, it is a book written for adults—particularly those adults who are educators, teacher educators, educational researchers, and educational leaders—so that we can begin to look at ourselves as part of the solution to the real crisis, the crisis of marginalization; and so that in the educational community we can reposition youth as knowledgeable producers and, specifically for the purposes of this book, as producers of multimodal texts and youth culture. As educators, we look at the possibility of bringing in powerful ways of working with youth and media—what we are calling critical media pedagogies—to improve academic development and meaningful social exchange.

Why critical media pedagogies? How can teaching media in high school English and social studies classrooms help to tackle major challenges in our educational system? First of all, we know that students are more motivated to participate in activities that are culturally and socially relevant to them, and our argument is that incorporating media education into academic subjects holds the possibility of increasing motivation and engagement to participate in core academic content. Quantitatively, at the very least, there is no doubt that new media are relevant to school-aged youth. The lives of America's city youth are saturated with multiple forms of media that include film, music, television, mobile media apps, and video game consoles; taken as a whole, youth spend the majority of their waking lives as consumers and producers of media (Ito et al., 2009). The power of new media in the lives of young people cannot be denied, and therefore, media education needs to be more effectively implemented into K–12 curricula in the United States (Beach, Campano, & Edmiston, 2010; Kist, 2005).

Other scholars have called for media education, but their versions of media education have largely entailed the study of media texts. While this is important, our critical pedagogy that literally frames the "media" in our approach recognizes the democratizing nature of media as facilitating modes of the production and distribution of youth counter-narratives. Through our critical pedagogy of media in core content areas, students may become media pedagogues who share critical information with large audiences via digital outlets.

Very few would deny that we are living in the midst of a digital media revolution. As we enter the second decade of the 21st century, our lives have been drastically changed by the ubiquity of cyberspace and the hegemony of new media tools such as laptop computers, netbooks, smartphones, PDAs (personal digital assistants), portable media players, tablets, e-readers, and digital video cameras. A whole new language and culture of production have been created, and our ways of communicating with one another have made the world a very different place, at least in the Western world in nations such as the United States. Given this communications revolution, which will have major implications for civic and professional life in the 21st century, we as educators will have to think differently about how we teach, the tools we use, and the products that we demand from our students. Particularly, we will have to re-imagine concepts such as pedagogy and literacy, and we will have to think and theorize how 21st century education will deal with media consumption and production across the K–12 spectrum and across the disciplines (Lievrouw, 2011). We can no longer afford to have our heads in the sand. Nor can we pretend that it's acceptable to have classrooms without computers and high-speed Internet access. The tools, however, are not the only answer. We must figure out how to incorporate these tools and technologies into our classroom instruction across the disciplines. In addition to providing a context for critical access to 21st century learning technologies, we also feel that a critical media education can help to intervene in the academic literacy underachievement that is present in most city centers, including in the schools where this research has been conducted. This book presents English and social studies classrooms that are sensitive to the changing nature of literacy at the dawn of the new media revolution.

As a field, we need to understand how media have been conceptualized and studied; we also need to understand the various ways that youth are practicing media, as well as how these practices are constantly changing and increasing in sophistication over time. Finally, we need practical examples of how classroom teaching can embrace these new media practices while also addressing disciplinary content and academic literacy development.

This book fills several important niches in the field. First of all, this book speaks directly to the emergent field of media education. At present, there are not many books that combine media studies and media education that try to integrate theory with pedagogical practice in city schools. This book pushes on conceptions of media education as empowering media production, but it also centers this theorizing within the analysis of actual classroom practice and work in non-classroom settings with youth. Additionally, there are not many books that explore the intersection of media production and content-specific instruction, specifically content-area instruction in city classrooms. Most of the potential audience of teachers who have an interest in media education are not going to be teaching special media or cultural studies classes; rather, they are going to have to find ways to incorporate media literacies into traditional core classes, and they are going to be doing this in a context that is often scripted or constrained. The educators who have co-authored this book have brought media literacies into these very spaces. The stories, we hope, are inspiring, but they are also pragmatic in that they outline how it is possible to develop a rigorous, standards-based, content-area curriculum that includes ample amounts of media production. Finally, the book is unique in that it moves from ethnography to classroom practice. That is, the data gathered on youth media production are used directly in the planning of classroom interventions.

The goals in this introduction are to (1) frame the problem, (2) introduce the potential of a critical media pedagogy in city schools and classrooms, and (3) provide an overview of the conceptual frames within which the book is situated. These frames include critical pedagogy, sociocultural learning theory, and media and cultural studies. With respect to the latter, the book pays particular attention to the emergent focus in cultural studies on youth as media producers (Lievrouw, 2011). With respect to the problems, we know a great deal about academic literacy underachievement in city centers. The discrepancies in academic literacy have serious and lasting effects on quality of life for individual students and whole communities. As the reauthorization of the Elementary and Secondary Education Act (ESEA) is debated in both houses of Congress, a great amount of focus is being placed on our inability to provide pathways to college for poor, ethnic minority, and inner-city populations (College Board, 2008; U.S. Department of Education, 2010). Improving academic literacy is a major step in the right direction toward improving college access. Students with high levels of academic literacy and high levels of engagement are likely to perform better in their content-area classes and on standardized exams. We also know something about the changing nature of literacy as we enter the dawn of the participatory media revolution. As literacy demands change in our technologically advancing society, literacy education also needs to change. This book addresses both of these fundamental problems in that it examines practices that increase academic literacy development and that incorporate new media technologies into content-area instruction in secondary classrooms. It further argues that drawing on new media literacies increases student motivation and engagement and makes connections between out-of-school literacies and classroom practice.

We also want to offer a definition of *critical pedagogy* as it is practiced across the school sites and youth engagement programs described in the book. As educators, we met to discuss the literature on critical theory and critical pedagogy as we simultaneously planned for our courses and programs. This first chapter reflects this conversation between theory and practice. We do this because we believe wholeheartedly that what is needed is not a media pedagogy for city education, but a critical media pedagogy. However, we also recognize that it is sometimes difficult to make connections between somewhat esoteric critical theory and the world of U.S. city classrooms in 2012. Toward these ends, we try to capture our honest conversations about the uses of critical pedagogy in today's classrooms, as well as the connections between critical pedagogy and media production.

ESSENTIAL QUESTIONS

As educators, we followed a process of collaborative teacher inquiry, wherein we asked critical questions about practice, collected information to determine whether we were being successful, and drew upon our analysis of the information we collected and the collective conversations to modify lessons and curricula. The final phase of this project is sharing what we have learned. The following questions have guided our collaborative project:

1. What is a critical media education? What can it look like in city classrooms in the humanities disciplines?
2. How are city youth participating in media today?
3. How can these practices be acknowledged and embedded into traditional academic content areas?
4. What are the various outcomes associated with critical media pedagogy in secondary English and social studies classes?

OUTLINE OF BOOK CHAPTERS

The second chapter will draw upon demographic and ethnographic data to explore the multiple ways that teens are consuming and producing new media during the first decade of the new millennium. Particular emphasis will be paid to cyberpunk culture, web design, social networking sites, Internet radio, blogging, text messaging, independent music production, and digital filmmaking. Our goal in this chapter is to draw from the work of New Literacy Studies, which uses ethnography to unpack the literacy and cultural production practices of working-class populations that have not been regarded as intellectuals or knowledge producers. As Raymond Williams, a key contributor to the Birmingham Centre of Contemporary Cultural Studies, comments, "culture is ordinary." And in moving from culture being the domain of the elite to being ordinary, we allow for the reality that ordinary people produce culture in powerful ways. In using ethnography, visual sociology, and semiotics to document and make sense of youth as media producers, we want to make the case that schools and classrooms should draw on these cultures of production as part of the development of affirming and culturally relevant pedagogical practices.

In Chapter 3, we introduce the readers to the sites of these projects: two secondary schools in southern California and a university–school partnership where youth use research and media production to tell powerful stories about their neighborhoods and schools. We briefly outline the rich history of the neighborhoods within which these schools reside and show the role mainstream media play in portraying these neighborhoods in ways that leave lasting imprints on the national imagination. We juxtapose these dominant media narratives about the cities and neighborhoods with a counter-narrative of indigenous media production from neighborhood residents. The latter narrative, read in songs, films, poems, and public murals, is one of togetherness, action, and pride. In this chapter, we will also present the school demographics and the data on academic achievement, high school completion, and college access. We underscore the disconnect between the history of production and activism in the communities with the history of underachievement at the school, and we set the context for sharing the stories of the teachers and the students who are involved in classroom interventions and extracurricular activities that facilitate the development of academic, critical, and new media literacies.

Chapter 4 explores critical media practices in a high school English classroom. This chapter, which features the classroom of Ms. Veronica Garcia, will detail the essential components of her teaching philosophy, key units, analysis of outcomes of units and strategies, and implications for the teaching profession. The chapter will begin with a discussion of the most critical and essential elements of Ms. Garcia's teaching philosophy, in order to understand the thinking behind how she engages and plans for students. These components include the use of the word "critical" in assignment titles, integration of popular culture and media, culturally relevant curriculum (i.e., books, materials, and resources), connection to the theme of the school's small learning community, and production of quality student work. Next, the chapter provides a description and analysis of four successful units for 9th-graders that she has used for several years in an English Language Arts course. These units include poetry, media and persuasion, literary response and analysis, and narrative. Each unit will include an overview and description of what students were required to do, the resources and materials they used, and examples of student work. Finally, this chapter will conclude with an analysis and reflection on the experience of teaching students with these strategies and units over time. It will discuss the idea of students as producers and intellectuals and how teachers can be "researchers" in the process, opening up new conversations and sharing publicly (with students) their work and curriculum units. This chapter also discusses how these critical elements of one's teaching philosophy have implications for strong, but also challenging, relationships with students, largely due to the personal stories and experiences that come out in students' work, discussions, and daily interactions both inside and outside of school.

Chapter 5 is an exploration into the curriculum and pedagogy of Roosevelt High School social studies teacher Mr. Jorge López. We examine his philosophy of teaching, his focus on popular culture and cultural studies, and their applications to the teaching of social studies. We also investigate how this plays out in several novel courses he designed, such as Cultural History and Popular Culture: The Latino and Black Experience in Urban America, Youth and Justice, and Sociology of Urban Youth and Education. In his courses, Mr. López's students learn to critique dominant social forces, such as popular culture, popular music, and its media outlets. Courses begin by building a foundation of knowledge through the historical and theoretical study of oppression and resistance to oppression and neocolonialism. Students develop a critical lens to examine history, culture, and their presence in urban Los Angeles. Courses culminate with a student-developed counter-hegemonic media project. The chapter also explores ways that Mr. López incorporates his ideas about the critical study of media into more traditional social studies using project-based media production in courses such as World History and U.S. History.

Chapter 6 is an exploration into the curriculum and pedagogy of Wilson High School social studies teacher Mr. Rudy Dueñas.

The chapter explores his philosophy of teaching and the genesis of the pan-ethnic studies program at Wilson High School that includes African American Studies, Asian American Studies, Mexican American Studies, and Latin American Studies. It takes a look at how Mr. Dueñas incorporates media production into this ethnic studies sequence, paying close attention to his focus on visual sociology, the use of images and art to teach about race and ethnicity, and his current project developing documentaries with his students on ancestral memories and healthy foodways. It also looks at the ways that Mr. Dueñas incorporates his ideas about the critical study of media into more traditional social studies courses such as U.S. History.

One of the things that became immediately clear was that much of the collective work with youth takes place in spaces that are not classrooms and, therefore, are often unaccounted for in the literature on effective pedagogies with youth. Specifically, many of the most powerful interactions with youth happen inside of structured learning environments that are not formal classrooms. While a major focus is to offer concrete examples of how media production plays out inside of traditional content-area courses, it would be a shame to lose the rich examples of additional work with students, so the last two chapters offer numerous examples of work that was undertaken with youth in what has been termed the "Third Space." Why are these third spaces so important? Schools are full of opportunities to work with young people, and many of these spaces—be it clubs or sports or societies or after-school programs—are hybrid spaces where young people make some of their most powerful connections to learning and school. The formal curriculum of school marginalizes these spaces by their very name (i.e., extracurricular), even though they are ripe with potential to provide the same kinds of opportunities for engagement, production, and learning as classrooms do. So the book chronicles several ways that the author team has taken advantage of these spaces to engage youth in media production.

Chapter 7 looks at several examples at Roosevelt and Wilson high schools: a MEChA club that employs critical drama as a social action strategy, an ART (Art of Revolutionary Teens) Club that uses murals as a form of community education, and a research club where youth used media to inform peers and administrators about important educational issues. The final section of Chapter 7 will show what is possible in "outside of school" spaces in terms of the extended development of multimodal artifacts. The section explores a 12-year, multi-school project directed by Mr. Morrell, called the Council of Youth Research, that involves city youth in collecting and disseminating research related to the conditions of city schools. Since 1999, these youth have conducted action research projects on life in schools and communities. They have conducted interviews; distributed surveys; and visited schools, neighborhood centers, and policy arenas. They have created research reports, news articles, blogs, essays, PowerPoint presentations, and digital documentaries. They have presented their work at Los Angeles City Hall, at universities, and at national research conferences throughout the United States. They have also disseminated their work virtually through blogs, Ning sites, Facebook, YouTube, and the UCLA Institute for Democracy, Education and Access (IDEA) website. They have been covered by local and national media such as CNN, the *Los Angeles Times*, KPCC, *La Opinion*, New America Media, and the *Los Angeles Daily News*, to name a few. Specifically, Chapter 7 will analyze the role of documentary filmmaking in the Youth Council's mission. How do the members of the Youth Council become digital filmmakers? What academic, new media, and civic literacies do they develop in this process? How do students involved in the Youth Council employ their digital documentaries in their action for social change?

What does this mean for secondary city education at the dawn of the 21st century? The goal in the concluding chapter is to show that even teachers with minimal instincts regarding new media literacies can bring them into classrooms in powerful ways. Chapter 8 also demonstrates that it is possible to think about infusing critical media education into all facets of the traditional secondary humanities curricula without losing a focus on academic literacy development or disciplinary content. Finally, it reaffirms the authors' commitment to critical pedagogy and empowering teaching that humanizes youth, while also setting high expectations and developing much-needed competencies for life and engagement in the 21st century. Toward these ends, it speaks to the need for building relationships and developing meta-narratives of schools as potential sites of either social reproduction or social change. No tools, in and of themselves, will lead to change in urban schools. That change will only come through teachers who draw on critical frameworks to create learning communities where the use of these tools becomes an empowering enterprise.

2 Youth and Critical Media Production in the 21st Century

Vignette 1: Oscar Grant

On January 1, 2009, police officers shot an unarmed 22-year-old named Oscar Grant in front of a crowd of passengers at a BART Station in Oakland, California. While tragic, the event, in and of itself, is not unique. Young African American males are shot by the police on occasion and often in the presence of witnesses. This case is unique and relevant to a conversation about media studies for several reasons. Many of the witnesses were carrying smartphones capable of capturing video footage, and dozens of cell phones recorded the arrest and alleged altercation that led to the shooting death of an unarmed and handcuffed arrestee. Immediately following the shooting, videos contradicting the officers' reports were released into the public domain. Several guerilla filmmakers sent their cell phone videos to news media, which began broadcasting these short films on major newscasts. Other mobile phone videos that were uploaded directly to the Internet went "viral," racking up millions of views and forcing a public response to the event.

Vignette 2: The Egyptian Uprising

When historians reflect on the so-named Arab Spring of 2011, they will no doubt begin with the Egyptian demonstrations that led to the ultimate departure of Hosni Mubarak, who had led the nation for 30 years. Near the end of the 18 days of protest, we will remember American journalists engaging the confident and victorious rebels at Tahrir (Liberation) Square, but the outcome was not always a foregone conclusion. At a much earlier point, when these youth were congregated under much more hostile conditions in relation to Mubarak's forces, videos began to circulate around the Internet that not only depicted the tremendous force of the group of "rebels" but also the violent repression of the protests by the government. Calls came from leaders throughout the world condemning violence against peaceful protesters. The strategic use of media served as leverage that ultimately allowed the protests to gain enough steam to topple the Egyptian government and fuel mass demonstrations in other countries such as Yemen, Syria, Bahrain, and Jordan.

How are youth participating in media today in their own spaces and on their own terms? What are the important skills and sensibilities that they gain through these activities? How are they, via their media participation, influencing the world around them? If, as educator John Dewey (1900) advocates, we are to build our curricula around the worlds of our students, then our challenge in developing powerful media curricula for the humanities is to understand the ways that many of our youth are currently producing and consuming media in out-of-school spaces. We say "many" of our youth (as opposed to "all") because we know that access to the media is still, in many ways, mediated by class and wealth. However, there are still myriad ways that youth are involved in the activities of consuming and producing media that seem important as a backdrop to the in-class and extended-time activities that we describe later in the book. So we begin our study as ethnographers and visual sociologists as we attempt to map out the terrain of youth media use through the first decade of the 21st century.

FRAMING THE ISSUE:
CRITICAL MEDIA PEDAGOGY IN THEORY AND PRACTICE

We draw on sociocultural theories of learning as we develop our own critical model that contains the following components:

1. *Learning must be active*—learners need to be out in the real world doing real things that matter to them and to others.
2. *Learning must be authentic*—whenever possible the tasks must have meaning and purpose.
3. *Learning must be participatory*—learning happens within a community that is multi-level and multi-aged if possible.
4. *Learning must be empowering*—learning must give students power to act differently upon the world, and they must be aware of how their learning in formal environments translates into power in academics, in the professional world, and in civic life.

A critical theory of learning embraces these tenets and builds upon community cultural wealth and students' intrinsic desire to enact social change to create learning spaces that are rigorous, relevant, participatory, authentic, and engaging of content—and of the social world.

Conceptually, our ideas regarding youth critical media production are guided by the idea of pedagogy as an act of empowerment (Freire, 1970). While much of the current work on youth media engagement doesn't deal explicitly with pedagogy, our work begins there. Specifically, we believe that a critical pedagogy of media inspires critical media production. Our project is interested in the act of media production, but we don't feel that producing media, in and of itself, necessarily constitutes critical activity. By contrast, we are explicitly interested in developing critical media pedagogies that result in the production of critical media. By critical media production, we intend to frame media production as an act of what Freire calls "problem posing." That is, we feel that students can use media artifacts such as blogs and digital films as a way to encourage dialogue about inequities in education and in society at large. Additionally, developing and distributing media as a tool of resistance is an act of *counter-hegemony* (Gramsci, 1971) in that the students are using the communications tools at their disposal to share competing narratives of their social context. These competing narratives, we argue, are often more authentic, more complex, more humane, and more compelling. One of the core tenets of critical pedagogies is that they reinforce the idea that students become producers (and, we would add, distributors) of valuable knowledge as part of the pedagogical act. Traditional education, to the contrary, often encourages working-class students to participate as uncritical consumers of state-sanctioned knowledge (Anyon, 1981; Freire, 1970).

Our work is also informed by cultural studies and the New Literacy Studies (NLS). New Literacy Studies, which emerged as a sub-discipline in the 1980s, build on the scholarship of the ethnography of communication (Gumperz & Hymes, 1972) to explore the multiple ways that humans use language and literacy powerfully in everyday cultural practice. Moving beyond the autonomous model of literacy, Street (1984) contends that literacies are multiple, cultural, and socially situated. The role of literacy researchers operating from an NLS perspective is not to reify hierarchies of literacy practice, but rather to reveal the complex ways in which historically marginalized groups negotiate traditional and new media literacies in the digital age.

Additionally, this work is guided by a critical theory of learning that challenges traditional interactions between teachers and students and between students and the world. Jean Lave (1996) reminds us that behind any theory of literacy is a theory of learning. Too often, however, the theories of learning prevalent in classrooms that serve the poor and historically marginalized portray students as passive receptacles of knowledge who demonstrate competency by regurgitating facts (Freire, 1970; Anyon, 1981; Oakes, 1985). Whether we are talking about low-tracked classes or under-resourced schools, learning is often reduced to rote memorization of information that will be tested. By contrast, in the workplace and in cultural activity, learning generally happens through authentic participation (Dewey, 1900; Lave & Wenger, 1991) and through apprenticeships, where more knowledgeable members guide novices through practice while yielding increasing responsibilities until expertise is reached (Lee, 2007; Rogoff, 1990).

With this framework in mind, we have sought out examples of how youth use media to convey critical information to their peers in ways that promote social awareness and social action. We also document the various traditional and new media literacies that are associated with these dynamic youth-initiated and youth-led communities of practice. Our hope is that we can begin to situate youth as powerful learners and teachers of media and as literate and conscientious beings that are capable of highly motivated and motivating literate activity. This re-envisioning of youth and their capabilities is essential to the pedagogical practices we describe in later chapters.

CULTURAL STUDIES AND YOUTH MEDIA PARTICIPATION IN THE ERA OF WEB 2.0

Reading Media

Even though Web 2.0 is largely defined by the media that youth are producing today, it is still important to consider all of the ways that youth continue to "read" media. We place *read* here in quotes because, while much of this reading involves the traditional decoding of print, youth are also interpreting visual signs such as photographs, digital films, webpages, advertisements, and video games, to name a few.

In working with our youth, we noted a number of important practices that involve reading in a traditional sense. Some of these practices include the following.

Reading email. Whether via social networking sites such as Facebook or Twitter, or through email providers such as Gmail, AOL, Yahoo!, or Mobile Me, most of our students have a way of sending electronic communications that resemble "letters" from previous generations.

Students send short messages to one another related to personal and academic concerns. Youth also use emails to communicate with distant family members and even their classroom teachers on occasion. Reading emails may also include processing advertisements sent to their inboxes from their favorite musical groups, television shows, and clothing brands. Many professional websites allow browsers to join email lists, where they can be kept abreast of the latest news related to their product. Youth also read information put out by advocacy groups that reach out to youth to inform them about social issues. Many students receive information about issues that matter to them via occasional email blasts that will encourage them to take action in their communities. Some examples include environmental action groups, groups that promote healthy living, and groups that represent political causes such as the passing of the DREAM Act. While this section is focused primarily on reading the media, we should also note that many of these email communications are written by youth for youth. This ensures that the messages are more accessible and more relevant.

Reading content on websites. Students who may participate in organizations or clubs or other activities and groups can also come into contact with various forms of educational information on the web. For example, students in the Council of Youth Research access demographic and educational data at the school, community, city, and state levels on education and U.S. Census websites. They learned how to read school scores on attendance, testing, and even budgets. They researched the biographies of individuals from the governor of California to the superintendent of the Los Angeles Unified School District (LAUSD). They regularly visit the websites of community-based organizations to learn about what resources exist in neighborhoods to serve students and their families. Some examples of websites that they have consulted include the U.S. Census Factfinder, the Department of Education, local school websites, and the websites of local community-based organizations.

Youth also interact with the online news media to keep informed about the latest news or breaking stories. Many young people stay connected to current events via online news outlets such as Yahoo!, AOL, and CNN.com. It is common for young people to read news stories online and then share these stories with other youth by pasting the link to the stories on their social media pages or via Twitter.

Reading electronic books on tablets and PDAs. In cities throughout the country, school districts are slowly beginning to transfer the use of textbooks to digital books now that Apple has moved to make them available for schools. Schools are trading in heavy, hardback textbooks for lightweight iPads for their students, and students in Communications, New Media, and Technology (CNMT) at Roosevelt High School are now reading website content in their classrooms using iPads and iPods. The school also received classroom carts of laptop computers for teachers to make literacy more engaging through the usage of media tools. In their history classes, students are using iPads to read news articles from multiple news websites to build literacy and learn to read the world. Reading text beyond the traditional paper print raises the level of interest among youth, both because most students have never used an iPad and because reading text from a screen connects with their high interest level in media technologies. In the classroom, students scrolled through articles, annotating in their notebooks, and making sense of the text through discussion using multiple literacy strategies.

"Reading" popular culture. Students learn the difference between being a critical consumer and being a passive consumer when they engage with different forms of popular culture. Students interact with popular culture symbols, messages, and individuals who represent these types of media every day at home, at school, with friends, and in just about every kind of space both inside and outside of school. Freire (1970) knew that individuals "read the world" before they "read the word." Students understand the world around them much better than adults do and just need opportunities to discuss it. For example, they "read" TV commercials, public service announcements, and advertisements via video and images. They watch music videos on television or the Internet from their phones or computers. They download and listen to music on their iPods, tablets, and smartphones. Even video games act as a way for students to digest popular culture on a daily basis. Students can become *critical* consumers rather than passive ones when they go a step further and learn how to break down and analyze an image, video, or advertisement through words, colors, object positions, and settings in the classroom. When they next discuss the effects of media on their lives, their worldview changes and grows into new perspectives about popular culture and consumerism.

Cyberpunk culture/hacking. When it comes to accessing music, film, or programs, young people know where to go to get it free of charge. There is an entire culture of youth sharing information, sites, and the steps needed to share multiple types of downloads with each other. Expensive video editing software such as Final Cut Pro can be easily shared and accessed in the cyberpunk/hacking network culture. Due to the growing accessibility of streaming copyrighted content, such as music, film, and software, Congress drafted two bills, the Stop Online Piracy Act (SOPA) and the Protect IP Act (PIPA), to counter the growing hacking and content-streaming Internet culture by limiting search engines, criminalizing the streaming of copyrighted material, and blocking access to many sites. In response, cyberactivists were quick to gather support from big media sites such as Facebook, Google, Wiki, and SoundCloud, flooding the email inboxes of members of Congress and protesting on Capitol Hill to defeat the proposed laws. However, similar laws continue to be proposed by world governments and are expected to make another comeback in the U.S. Congress. International hacking groups such as Anonymous have become a huge threat to government institutions. The leaderless hacktivist organization goes undetected as it targets government and corporate websites, such as the recent attack on the website of the San Francisco Bay Area Rapid Transit (BART) in response to cell phone censorship during the organizing and protesting against BART and police for the killing of a homeless man. Anonymous released the statement, "We are your citizens, we are the people, and we do not tolerate oppression from any government agency." A recent Anonymous video expressed its discontent with the National Defense Authorization Act (NDAA), which it viewed as a constitutional rights attack. Members of the hacking subculture see themselves as aligned with the mission of WikiLeaks, the Occupy movement, and other global protest movements that address the needs of the oppressed, fight against abuses of power, and advocate for freedom of information. Young people post video messages from these groups on social media sites and are captivated by their approach to addressing injustice.

Critical Uses of Mobile Media

The use of mobile media devices has become a powerful tool in the hands of young people. Globally, citizens have used them to communicate their struggles, organize movements, and stay informed. Mobile devices such as smartphones with Internet access or iPods with Wi-Fi accessibility are commonly used by youth. Youth mobile media literacy can foster greater educational opportunities in the classroom, such as student engagement in social media sites to elevate critical thinking and social consciousness. Mr. López uses Twitter to keep his students up to date on news that involves social and political issues and provides students with an opportunity to write reports for additional points in class; some students have created Twitter accounts to follow his tweets. For example, in his World History class, students were studying world revolutions, where they learned and compared nonviolent methods applied in the Egyptian revolution and the Occupy movement, specifically looking at the use of mobile devices and social media sites, such as Twitter and Facebook. Mr. López used his mobile phone in class to demonstrate how to use Twitter. Students read tweets from Egyptian and Occupy LA activist profiles. Students felt empowered when learning that they, too, could become reporters using social media sites. Mr. López exposed students to applications such as UStream, which allows users to use their mobile phone cameras to stream video footage. Throughout the school year, students indicated they began re-tweeting and re-posting socially and politically charged articles and messages for their Facebook friends and followers, a drastic shift from prior content in comments and postings. Students began consuming media critically—many modeling the use of their mobile devices on the tactics of Occupy activists and Egyptian revolutionaries. Many social justice educators are already using mobile devices as a means of staying informed and connected to justice movements. It is equally important to teach students how to critically consume mobile media devices to develop critical consciousness, engage civically with the world, and participate in the global dialogue. Mr. López believes that it is powerful when youth critically engage in using their mobile media devices to keep their peers informed of news in their community and issues that most matter to them.

Educators can guide students to local and alternative media profiles to follow through their phones in sites such as Twitter and Facebook. Creating curriculum for students on the critical use of mobile phones to keep fellow community members informed and advocating for social justice puts the power of change in the hands of youth. In Mr. López's advisory class, he ran a workshop called Know Your Rights, which responded to the climate of heavy police harassment, illegal searches, and abuse of power in Boyle Heights. Mr. López reminded students that their mobile devices are tools that they have the right to use to photograph, video record, and report police carrying out their activity. Youth can become vigilant about their community by using mobile devices to document injustice and by knowing how to report to social justice media and organizations. During the Black Power movement, organizations such as the Black Panther Party for Self Defense carried guns to demonstrate that they were prepared to defend their community, leading to an increase of police repression. Today, mobile devices are being used by social justice organizations and activists to prevent police brutality, sending the message that "the world is watching." YouTube videos that instructed media users how to strategically use mobile devices and video cameras to monitor police during protests and the Occupy movement continue to be re-posted and shared on social media sites such as Twitter and Facebook. Mobile devices can become powerful weapons in the hands of the marginalized and can give voice to the voiceless. Teaching students the power of mobile devices can transfer to raising critical consciousness among youth—through reading text from powerful leaders and authors to the feeling of empowerment every time a young person produces his/her own messaging or re-tweets an article or YouTube video he/she is passionate about.

Social Networking

Social networking sites such as Twitter, Facebook, YouTube, and Google+ are providing millions of people with a web-based space to interact with each other over the Internet, creating online communities where users can share their ideas, communicate, share videos and photos, and organize events for an array of interests. Social networking sites are centered on the user's profile. This profile allows users to personalize the site according to their interests and purpose. Members of the global community across geographic, economic, and political regions are connecting through social networking sites for political purposes, and educational goals, or simply to connect with friends and family.

Alla Zollers (2009) identifies social network sites as "contested terrain" due to their commercial nature and the potential for narcissistic use by people. However, she points out that sites can serve political uses. Douglas Kellner and Gooyong Kim (2010) argue that applying critical pedagogy in social networking sites has the potential to create a more democratic, participatory, and social justice–oriented role for such sites. Mr. López uses sites such as Facebook and Twitter to have students read politically and culturally charged articles. Many of the posts include empowerment quotes and links to videos and documentaries found on YouTube. Similarly, the students from the Council of Youth Research have also developed Facebook and YouTube accounts where they share their critical activities with a larger public. We believe that social networking sites can become spaces of action where students can share their films or guide other students to critical discovery through various links. Young people who resist hegemonic forces are eager to distribute counter-narratives to other youth and are driven by what Freire (1970) refers to as "radical curiosity." Youths' curiosity to know and their desire to change unjust conditions propels them to use whatever tools are at their disposal, including social networking sites, to engage in the fight for social justice.

Infrastructure Design, Programming

Digital filmmaking. In this flip-cam and YouTube generation, the average person can shoot, edit, and distribute digital film to an international audience. After all, who hasn't seen viral videos of insane sports highlights, daredevil activities, or embarrassing gaffes that happened to be caught on film? Many of these short YouTube clips are only lightly edited, and their artistic merit leaves much to be desired. However, they are representative of a revolution in digital communication and belie a much more serious movement of youth filmmaking that has aesthetic value and social impact. The film "A Girl Like Me" comes to mind. Shot in New York City by then 16-year-old Kiri Davis, the digital documentary chronicles the challenges young African American girls face dealing with racial and gender challenges in contemporary American society. The short film contains multiple excerpts from interviews with teenage girls, and the filmmaker also re-conducts the "doll test," where African American preschoolers must choose between black and white dolls and explain their choices. Just as in the famous Clark and Clark experiment (which was instrumental in the *Brown v. Board of Education of Topeka* decision), the preschoolers overwhelmingly chose the white doll and ascribed to it characteristics such as good, nice, and smart. The film has been aired on HBO, *Good Morning America,* and the AFI/Discovery Channel Documentary festival.Ms. Davis even has her own Wikipedia entry!

Youth are developing and demonstrating myriad literacy skills via their participation in digital filmmaking. Young people are learning the skills of shooting and editing movies as they are now able to transfer raw footage from their cell phones, flip-cams, and more sophisticated high-definition (HD) cameras to computer programs such as iMovie, Final Cut Pro, or Adobe Premiere, where they can edit these clips into montages or short cuts with seamless transitions, adding graphics, music, and credits. While there are still many raw footage clips displayed on YouTube, an analysis of the content produced by young people also reveals that young people are developing more sophisticated filming skills.

Youth are also learning about various formats of saving and sharing the large files that are needed to create and distribute films. They understand that digital files have to be compressed into Quicktime or other readable formats before they can be uploaded to sites such as Facebook, Google+, and YouTube. Once their videos are posted on these sites, young people know how to link or embed videos into their posts on social media sites, blogs, and webpages. Most social media sites and blogs such as Wordpress give the embedded videos a professional look that, just a decade ago, would only have been possible for highly compensated web designers to achieve. As an example, with the sudden passing of pop star Whitney Houston in 2012, millions of her young fans began posting photos and video clips of their favorite Whitney moments. Built into this virtual memorial are several important skills—such as knowing how to search through various sites that contain Whitney Houston videos, how to copy and paste URLs of favorite websites, how to copy and embed code to include the videos seamlessly on webpages and social media sites, and how to add personal tributes and tag friends in posts to spread the word to others.

Music production. Young people are using music production software as it has become more accessible and are posting their musical productions on websites such as SoundCloud to reach a potentially unlimited audience with potentially unlimited exposure. Not too long ago, producing music required the use of studios and expensive equipment, but now, by using new media tools, talented youth who do not have the means to use a music studio can now produce music from their home computer. Music production is becoming more accessible to young people as applications such as Music Studio or SynthStation, which transform the iPad, iPhone, or iPod touch into a portable music production studio for mobile music creation, continue to be developed and downloaded. It is not uncommon for youth musicians to record their music using software such as Garageband, touchAble, or Fruity Loops. They can then use social media outlets like Facebook, Google+, and Twitter to market their bands. Sites such as Sonicbids and Reverbnation allow musicians to create electronic press kits (EPKs) that can be sent to prospective agents, venue owners, and record labels. These young musicians now also have the power to sell their music directly to the public through iTunes, Rhapsody, Napster, and other virtual outlets. Youth are also able to film videos that they distribute virtually through YouTube and other Internet sites. Most of these services are free or charge only nominal fees.

The independent music industry has taken advantage of the fluency with participatory media to grow a new generation of music consumers. During the decade where he ran a record label, Mr. Morrell witnessed a proliferation in the number of young people who began to promote and distribute music in the early 2000s via social media sites such as MySpace, which included music players for artists who could upload music in mp3 format and then visitors could come and listen to the music. In a later version, MySpace actually allowed artists to sell their music via their MySpace pages. MySpace was just one among the first generation of special media sites that promoted the sharing of music that would not be found on major record labels. Other specialized music pages include iTunes, Rhapsody, Reverbnation, and Pandora (which allows youth the opportunity to create their own radio stations).

Art production. Art production is a powerful form of media; images created by artist Shepard Fairey, such as the famous Hope poster of President Obama, were used to launch the 2008 Obama campaign by engaging the younger generation. The Urban Art movement has been on the rise in the last few years and has become part of popular culture. Films such as "Exit Through the Gift Shop" or "Bomb It" document the street art movement of urban cities throughout the world. Street artists from Europe, such as Banksy or Invader, are featured in films and in street art books. Bookstores carry sections of urban art/ graffiti art, and major museums are now having exclusive street art exhibits. Los Angeles's Museum of Contemporary Art (MOCA) featured a large exhibit of urban art in 2011 called *Art in the Streets.* According to the museum, this exhibit attracted more than 200,000 visitors, marking the highest exhibition attendance in museum history. It featured the work of hundreds of street artists throughout the world, including Los Angeles artists RETNA, RISK, and CHAZ BOJORQUEZ. The production styles take on multiple forms, including art installations, graffiti, brush on canvas, stencil art, and poster pasting. The work of artist JR, who calls himself an "urban artivist," are on view not only on the walls of the museum, but also in downtown Los Angeles and even on the LA River. JR takes pictures of people and prints huge portraits to paste on city walls, reaching communities that might not go to museums while projecting the human face and promoting humanity.

The work of urban artists can be seen in all media spaces—printed in books and magazines, in social media sites and videos, and in public spaces—making the medium accessible to all communities. Throughout Los Angeles, different forms of art can be seen on its walls, making the city a canvas of expression, where its members become artistic participants or public art consumers, analyzing the messages and simply enjoying the art form.

The mural, another form of public art that has been in Los Angeles for generations and was born on the walls of the Eastside in the 1970s, continues to live and flourish. In Boyle Heights, Roosevelt Art Club students learned from community public artist Raul Gonzalez the power of images in a workshop, in preparation for painting their next mural on the walls of the Eastside. Gonzalez conveyed to youth that public art and wall painting has played a meaningful role historically. Today, youth are taking on a meaningful role through image production; Gonzalez highlighted their responsibility to the public and to their community as public artists and muralists. Art production involves youth in the process of critical inquiry, in which they must analyze their world, engage in dialogue, and uncover community issues that need to be addressed or elements of their culture that need to be celebrated using images. In turn, critical youth artists become learners and teachers who use the production of public art to educate community members, build unity, and raise consciousness.

CONCLUSION

Whether they are taking photographs on their mobile phones and uploading them to their Facebook pages, or tweeting from their tablets, and no matter whether the media content youth are creating and distributing is of professional quality, there is no denying that (1) youth are participating in new media in powerful and creative ways, and (2) these cultural activities hold tremendous possibilities for classroom instruction in the humanities. Students must be given more credit by educators for their media literacy skills and more opportunities to use them in the classroom. In our brief exploration of the ways that our youth are involved in media, we not only affirmed our original hypothesis about the relevance of media education in formal classroom instruction, but we were also reminded of the generativity and everyday brilliance of young people, and of their power to weave together the narratives of their lives with multimodal threads of texts, still images, "film," and music.

3 The Neighborhoods, the Schools, the Projects, and the Study

Waiting for Superman No More

It is only March, but the main auditorium of the UCLA Downtown Labor Center is sweltering. Two archaic fans blow recycled hot air through the packed auditorium. Their melodic hum and the cracked doors and windows are a reminder of the elevated temperature. Nearly 200 parents, students, school personnel, district administrators, and members of the local media sit attentively in folding chairs for 90 minutes of presentations from the Council of Youth Research, a decade-long project involving student researchers from select high schools throughout the city. Each of the five high school groups has created a PowerPoint presentation and a 1-minute digital video Public Service Announcement (PSA) related to their theme, a Quality Education for All of California's Students. The Roosevelt group, one of the first to present, galvanizes the audience with talk of enlightened students serving as their own superheroes. Early in their presentation, the students show a clip from the movie "Waiting for Superman." In this clip, Daisy, a 5th-grader, is running across an East LA elementary school playground with her classmates. As she glides in slow motion across the screen, looking to her left and right at her young competitors, the narrator discusses the odds of Daisy receiving a quality education if she is forced to attend her local high school, Roosevelt, which is labeled by the film as a dropout factory. In the end of the clip, Daisy loses the race and we are saddened at the thought that this young girl has been sentenced to attend her horrible neighborhood schools. Indeed, in the film, Daisy's parents are trying to enroll her in a charter school, but their attempts are futile because her number isn't called in the lottery for admission to the local KIPP School. As she drives home from the lottery with her dad, Daisy is saddened, as are we (as the captive audience), because her fate is ostensibly sealed.

The five Roosevelt students respond to this critique of their school by putting themselves forward as a counter-narrative. They refer to themselves as smart, dynamic, technologically inclined, academically literate, and civically engaged, and they are adamant about not needing a "Superman" in their lives. Their 15-minute PowerPoint presentation deals with the social and physical ecology of schools. They speak to the real differences in the quality of life at campuses that serve the affluent versus those that serve the working class. They advocate for equity in funding and in school resources, but they also point toward the active resistance and the struggle for justice that continues at their school and others like it. At the end of their presentation, they open their dress shirts to reveal Superman t-shirts underneath, and in unison, they announce, "We are our own superheroes!" The media-enhanced presentation is captivating, powerful, and inspiring. A national media outlet interviews several of the Roosevelt students, and their story is featured in an online news story by Channel One, a cable station targeted toward K–12 schools.

We have all worked with the Roosevelt students, and we have now seen this presentation given to multiple audiences throughout the country. The students are empowered and successful. Three of the graduating seniors from this group received competitive scholarships to some of the most elite universities in the nation. All of the seniors graduated from high school and moved on to postsecondary education. Each of these young women and men are proud of what they have accomplished, as are we. But it is difficult to escape the feelings of revulsion each time the clip from the movie is shown. As we talk about the movie and the work of the Council of Youth Researchers in preparation for writing this book, we situate it alongside numerous other portrayals of East Los Angeles, most of them negative. Most of them point toward violence, drugs, abuse, and failure. The schools, the neighborhoods, and the residents are treated as monoliths—as powerless and as deficits.

We recognize the challenge of presenting neighborhoods and schools that have had problems while also showing the resiliency, the potential, and the amazing cultural production that are a part of these neighborhoods' histories. East Los Angeles is home to a tradition of action for social change; its artwork adorns the walls of schools, cafés, and community centers, and its media production has spoken to international audiences for nearly a century. East Los Angeles is also home to four high schools that feature wonderful teachers and students who are, in our estimation, superheroes.

So, in what follows we attempt to present the challenges, the triumphs, and the possibilities in our brief introduction to the Boyle Heights and El Sereno neighborhoods of East Los Angeles and to the high schools (Roosevelt and Wilson) that they are home to. It is our hope to create a human portrait of two All-American neighborhoods and their hard-working schools that struggle against the odds to provide an equitable and humanizing education to their students.

BOYLE HEIGHTS

Boyle Heights, the home of Roosevelt High School, is a vibrant neighborhood with a long history in Los Angeles. Its history dates back to the late 18th century, when the land was known as Paredon Blanco, or "White Bluffs." The land was populated by Mexican families; soon after the U.S.–Mexican War, Anglo immigrants began to populate Los Angeles. Andrew A. Boyle, an Irish immigrant who came to California during the gold rush, purchased land in Paredon Blanco and began to manufacture wine from his vineyards. After Boyle's death, his daughter, Maria Elizabeth Boyle, and her husband, William Henry Workman, inherited the land and renamed it Boyle Heights. During the economic boom of the 1880s, while Workman was mayor of Los Angeles, Boyle Heights became a desirable community for middle- and upper-middle-class families who built and settled in Victorian homes, which today are scattered and visible throughout the neighborhood. Many of the homes today are subdivided into rental units, where many of our students reside. In the early 1900s, wealthy families began to move out of Boyle Heights due to the growing industrial area and freight yards built by railroad tracks near the LA River. As wealthy families moved to the west side of the city, working-class and immigrant families moved to Boyle Heights and South LA, where industrial sites were developing. Both communities became the two areas in Los Angeles that did not have racially discriminatory housing restrictions; as a result, between the 1920s and 1940s, Boyle Heights became one of the most diverse American communities, with settlements of Jewish, Japanese, African American, Mexican, and Russian immigrant families. Historic synagogues and Buddhist temples still stand, reminding us of the rich cultural history of the community. During World War II, Jewish families began to migrate out of Boyle Heights and into Westside communities that had lifted racial restrictions on Jews. Japanese American families were forced into internment camps; thus, Boyle Heights became a predominantly Mexican American community after the war.

Postwar Boyle Heights saw an increase in Mexican American families, many of them farm workers who came to the United States under the Bracero Program during World War II. After the war, most of the families moving into the Westside—including the Fairfax district, Hollywood, and the San Fernando Valley—were wealthy Jews new to southern California. Boyle Heights Jews who settled during the 1920s were mostly from working-class backgrounds. Many had union backgrounds and wanted to create a civic-minded neighborhood and "instill a spirit of working together across ethnic lines" (Villa & Sanchez, 2005). During the mid-1950s, Boyle Heights had more than 100 coordinating councils, 50 community centers and associations, and more social workers than most communities (Villa & Sanchez, 2005). At this time, Mexican Americans constituted about half of the Boyle Heights population. New housing restrictions in Los Angeles during this era redefined whites, broadening the term "Caucasian race" to include Jews and eastern Europeans, who were allowed to settle in "white-only" neighborhoods as a result (Villa & Sanchez, 2005). Mexican American families and multiracial communities were excluded from federal government mortgage assistance. Communities of color in Los Angeles were socially marginalized and excluded from the postwar economic boom, which contributed to the anger and protests that occurred during the 1960s in Watts and in the Chicano Eastside (Davis, 2006). Mexican American veterans of World War II were excluded from many of the benefits that white GIs were receiving, such as housing assistance for new homes. It is important to note that although housing discrimination was outlawed by the Supreme Court in 1948, real estate agents, property owners associations, and lending companies continued to practice housing discrimination in Los Angeles until the 1970s (Villa & Sanchez, 2005). The lack of opportunities and housing access in Los Angeles for Mexican immigrant families contributed to the overcrowding of single-family homes in Boyle Heights. Today, students live in similarly crowded conditions because Boyle Heights continues to be a community open to new immigrants from Mexico and Central America.

The marginalization and racism experienced by the Boyle Heights community, and Mexican American families in particular, gave rise to the Eastside Chicano movement of the 1960s. Mexican Americans were fed up with continuing inequality. Many World War II Mexican American veterans returned from the war to face the same inequality and racism that existed before the war. Veterans who had risked their lives felt entitled to a more equitable and democratic society for their families and their country. The GI Bill provided economic access to higher education and as a result, the number of educated Chicanos increased in the Eastside. Access to academic literacy enabled young people in the Eastside to create social justice organizations and build a social consciousness in the minds of their community members. Fresh in the memory of the Eastside were the "Zoot Suit riots," in which police and military personnel brutalized young Chicanos in LA during World War II. Police repression and the demonization of black and brown youth by the press and City Council continued even after the war. The Boyle Heights community was outraged by Operation Wetback in 1954, which was launched by the Immigration and Naturalization Service. Jewish and Mexican Boyle Heights community members organized against deportations and raids (Villa & Sanchez, 2005). Similarly, today, Boyle Heights community activists and undocumented "Dreamer" students are organizing in the national movement against massive deportations that are taking place.

Inequality, marginalization, poverty, and a lack of access to a good education gave way to the Chicano movement. Young people created organizations like the United Mexican Americans Students (UMAS) and the Brown Berets, who were modeled after the Black Panther Party for Self Defense and dedicated themselves to protecting the community from police brutality and repression. Young people from the Eastside, in continuing the historical tradition of Boyle Height's civic minded-ness and service, developed solidarity with marginalized communities and people throughout America to build social justice for their community members. A new Chicano consciousness was being born, and communities were empowered through critical consciousness, indigenous identity, "carnalismo," and political engagement. The Chicano community, as with other communities of color, found empowerment in learning, self-reflection, and critical literacy. Young and old came together and learned the world through the word. Students knew that change, liberation, and justice could be achieved if all people learned their cultural history and identity and understood America's hegemonic systems of oppression. In 1968, high school students in Eastside schools organized a student strike and walked out of schools to demand a quality K-12 education, access to higher education, Mexican American studies, and cultural understanding and respect from school faculty. At the same time, Chicano students in Los Angeles community colleges and universities were organizing to increase recruitment of students of color and the establishment of Chicano studies departments. In the fall of 1968, the demands resulted in the nation's first Mexican American Studies department at California State University Los Angeles, located in the Eastside (Muñoz, 2007). Quickly, the number of students from the Eastside attending colleges and universities increased.

By August 1970, the Brown Berets and the Movimiento Estudiantil de Chicanos de Aztlan (MEChA) organized the first major Mexican

American demonstration against the war in Vietnam (Muñoz, 2007). The demonstration, known as the Chicano Moratorium, drew more than 20,000 people in solidarity with the Chicano anti-war movement from the entire Southwest. The East Los Angeles march ended with a police-provoked riot and the killing of three Mexican Americans; one of them was Ruben Salazar, a prominent *Los Angeles Times* journalist who reported on behalf of the Mexican American community. Every year, a commemorative Chicano Moratorium march, which attracts many community members, organizers, artists, and anti-war activists, is organized in the Eastside. The 1970s also witnessed a rise of socially and culturally conscious mural art in Boyle Heights and throughout East Los Angeles. Unfortunately, the 1970s also experienced a decrease in student activism as "new student organizations emerged that were more career-oriented, emphasizing individual advancement" (Muñoz, 2007, p. 104).

Boyle Heights is witnessing a cultural renaissance influenced by urban art, political consciousness, cultural indigenous identity, and a desire to build community and create a more just society. The East LA/ Boyle Heights scene is home to community poets, artists, organizers, and activists. Here, 1st Street features multiple art galleries and community centers—such as the media center Centro de Communicacion Comunitaria, Corazon del Pueblo, and Self-Help Graphics—that provide free workshops for youth to develop their voice, identity, and cultural expression through multiple forms of arts and media. Community and media centers consistently host community poets of all ages, art exhibits, and musical performers, who eloquently express the voice of the indigenous, urban, and socially conscious Chicano/a and Latino/a people. Benefit art, poetry, and music shows are always present in Boyle Heights, demonstrating support to undocumented students, immigrants, and solidarity with Raza, youth from numerous communities and states that are facing attacks from conservative forces. Boyle Heights youth and community members use Internet radio and social media outlets, like Twitter and Facebook, to communicate and organize upcoming community-building and solidarity and culture-raising events, along with keeping each other informed through news articles and YouTube links. During the late 1960s, college and high school students from the Eastside came together to politicize and organize Boyle Heights, and students from Roosevelt High and Wilson High continue to interact in spaces of empowerment, such as Corazon del Pueblo or the Proyecto Jardin community garden, where older Chicano/as can be seen running workshops for youth or performing spoken word together.

Roosevelt High School

Boyle Heights is home to Roosevelt High School, which was founded in 1922. In 2007, Roosevelt was identified as the most populated high school west of the Mississippi and also one of the most crowded. Because of the overcrowding, Roosevelt operated on a year-round system, with students assigned to one of three tracks, until 2010 when the school switched back to a traditional calendar and adopted a small-school model. Mr. López, who has taught at Roosevelt since 2002, now serves as one of the lead teachers for the school of Communications, New Media, and Technology (CNMT).

Roosevelt High is also one of the oldest, most significant, and most talked about schools in the city and the district. Among its alumni are some of the most visible Latino leaders and celebrities in the city's history. The current mayor of Los Angeles champions Roosevelt as one of his partnership high schools. A sense of pride and community pervades the campus. There are many student clubs, the walls are covered with murals, and the teachers' classroom walls are adorned with posters of famous leaders and activists. It feels good to be on the campus of Roosevelt High, but gazing back across the river at the skyline and the skyscrapers of downtown, something feels amiss, as if a covenant has been broken.

As is the case with many schools in the city of Los Angeles, Roosevelt is highly segregated, with a majority Latino/a population (nearly 99%). During the 2008–2009 academic year, it enrolled 4630 students with the following ethnic breakdown: White: 0.2%, African American: 0.2%, Hispanic: 98.7%, Asian: 0.2%, Filipino: 0.2%, American Indian: 0.1%, Pacific Islander: 0.0%, and Multi: 0.4% (Ed-Data, 2011). One-third (33.7%) of these students were classified as English Language learners, and 83.2% qualified for free and reduced lunch (as opposed to 52.6% for the state of California).

Academic Achievement at Roosevelt High

Graduation rates are reported in many different ways. The college opportunity ratio (COR) is a three-number figure that tells how many students graduate and how many pass the courses required for admission to California State Universities (CSU) and campuses in the University of California (UC) system *compared to each 100 students enrolled as 9th-graders.* For example, a COR of 100:90:50 means that for 100 9th-graders, 4 years later, 90 had graduated, and 50 had passed the courses required for admission to CSU and UC. The Institute for Democracy Education and Access reports the COR for all of California's high schools and for African American, Latino, and American Indian students who are under-represented in California's colleges. For the class of 2009, the COR for the state of California was 100:67:26. By comparison, the COR for Roosevelt (Theodore) Senior High was 100:35:6 (http://idea.gseis.ucla.edu/educational-opportunity-report/2011/).

Community members and activists in Boyle Heights began referring to the number of students not graduating as their disappearance rate. According to the college opportunity ratio, the disappearance rate at Roosevelt High School is 65%. Students and members of a local community organization have been working diligently for district and school reform. In the early 2000s, they worked to institute a requirement that all courses in the district be college-entrance requirements, essentially eliminating remedial classes (Rogers & Morrell, 2011). They also worked to ease the overcrowding in the school by forcing the school board to build additional schools in the neighborhood. These changes have been positive, reducing the school's population and allowing Roosevelt High to revert to a traditional calendar from a year-round calendar for the first time in a generation. However, the school still faces the challenge of keeping students in the educational pipeline and offering a curriculum that is both engaging and relevant to its students, one that will provide them with the skills that they need to successfully navigate high school and the postsecondary world of education, work, and citizenship.

The School of Communications and New Media Technology

In 2002, Linda Darling-Hammond led the School Redesign Network at Stanford University and published a booklet on ten features that make good small schools. The project was funded by the Gates Foundation, which from 2002 to 2008 invested more than $150 million to convert 23 underperforming New York high schools to 216 small schools (Blume, 2011). Also in 2002, the U.S. Department of Education began providing grants for large high schools to convert to Small Learning Communities (SLCs), a model similar to the Small Schools grants that the Bill and Melinda Gates Foundation was offering to schools. Unlike New York and Chicago, which were converting to small schools, the Los Angeles Unified School District began launching the Small Learning Communities (SLCs) model in its large high school sites. By 2007, Mr. López and teachers at Roosevelt High felt that the SLC model did not provide the autonomy that small schools offered. Many teachers called for a system modeled on the scholarship of Linda Darling-Hammond, whose work on small schools called for democratic decision making, multicultural and anti-racist teaching, authentic curriculum, personalization, and performance-based assessments. She argued that the traditional aged, factory-model school system approach to education is not working and has been failing our students' learning and success potential. In her publications, she asserts:

> A growing number of educators and policymakers believe that existing assembly-line schools that inhibit our students' and teachers' potential need to be replaced by smaller schools that are better designed to support teaching and learning. And we have evidence that small schools are indeed better for our children: All else equal, they produce higher achievement, lower dropout rates, greater attachment, and more participation in the curricular and extracurricular activities that prepare students for productive lives. There is real potential for the current small schools movement to transform the educational landscape in America for the better (Darling-Hammond, 2002, p. iii).

In 2007, the small-schools movement hit Boyle Heights, and community organizations InnerCity Struggle and the Boyle Heights Learning Collaborative began to organize with teachers, students, and parents to mobilize an initiative to create a small-schools model at Roosevelt High School. Mr. López was among the teachers at Roosevelt who were looking for a model that would provide autonomy in budgets, staffing, scheduling, curriculum and assessments, and governance. Teachers felt that a small-school environment of about 500 students, rather than 5000, along with autonomy in these areas, would set a platform to create a more personalized education to support the lives of students and raise academic achievement.

In 2007, the city's mayor, Antonio Villaraigosa, created a nonprofit organization, the Partnership for Los Angeles Schools (PLAS), to manage underperforming schools, with the goal of raising academic achievement and graduation rates. The PLAS met with Boyle Heights teachers and organizers to gain further autonomy from the school district and create a "Family of Schools," where PLAS would manage and support Roosevelt High and all its feeder schools, both middle and elementary. Community school parents and teachers voted for PLAS to manage some of the Boyle Heights schools. Soon, PLAS began to facilitate the process to convert Roosevelt into seven small schools modeled after the reform approach, making Roosevelt High the first large comprehensive public high school in Los Angeles to become independent small schools. PLAS guided the faculty in making the transition and provided support in several areas, including Single Plan for Student Achievement and budgets, to name a few.

Mr. López helped develop the school of Communications, New Media, and Technology (CNMT). The school's mission is to prepare all students for college, career, and civic engagement. The small school has a social justice and community schooling approach, with the goal of connecting student learning to college and careers in its thematic emphasis, using an approach known as Linked Learning. CNMT's community-school model works to reach out to university, industry, and community partners to provide students with academic and social support. The goal of the small school is not only to build social capital—networks of people and community resources—but also to emphasize the many forms of community capital and cultural wealth (Yosso, 2005). CNMT's usage of Yosso's six types of capital (aspirational, linguistic, familial, social, navigational, and resistance) within the small school and curriculum provides students with the tools, assets, skills, contacts, and mind-set to navigate through multiple institutional systems of oppression.

CNMT's mission is guided and informed through research, educational theory, and critical pedagogy. In curriculum and instruction, CNMT chose an inquiry- and project-based learning approach that uses media and technology literacies to develop communications skills that students need to succeed academically, think critically, and confront real-world problems throughout life.

CNMT's vision is to prepare graduates to succeed in college, pursue meaningful careers, and become civic participants of our democracy. Students learn the social responsibility of being communicators and producers of knowledge of the world by making their voices heard through discussions, projects, presentations, civic engagement, and media and technology exhibitions. Through inquiry-based instruction interwoven throughout multiple academic disciplines, students develop critical thinking skills while discovering their capacity to effect positive change in their lives, their community, and the world. Mr. López believes, "curriculum must be culturally relevant, address the lives of students, and include an underlying theme of social justice." His teaching philosophy follows the culturally relevant pedagogy of Gloria Ladson-Billings (1995), who suggests that teachers who implement pedagogy that draws from the social contexts of the lives of their students will create a richer learning environment that is engaging and student centered.

Student voice is at the center of CNMT's small school, and it is achieved through teacher-developed curriculum that is student centered, interdisciplinary, and thematic. Students develop their voice by using media production to communicate about relevant social issues. Using skills in research, speech, computer technology, and new media literacies, students share their developed products and findings with the school and community. Students also have multiple leadership opportunities through internships, clubs, and service-learning projects.

EL SERENO

Like Boyle Heights, El Sereno, the home of Woodrow Wilson High School, is a neighborhood with a strong identity and history. A drive through the city streets features views of historical murals and local shops that cater to the people's ethnic diversity. Signs are just as likely to be in Spanish as in English. Men sell fruit on street corners to passersby, who exchange money out of moving cars. Elderly women walk together, some pushing strollers carrying children who must be their grandchildren or great-grandchildren. The streets are named (or renamed) after famous heroes and activists; their spirit is juxtaposed with signs of urbanization and urban poverty. McDonald's and other major corporations are frequent haunts, and many of the local businesses and residences show the effects of neglect and decay. Still, it is a vibrant neighborhood filled, on any given day, with pedestrians who seem at home, even in a city where no one walks. The word "community," in its truest sense, comes to mind. Its high school sits atop a hill that offers spectacular views of the city on a clear day, prompting questions about the relationship of this school to this neighborhood and this city. How will the average student interact with those magnificent buildings over the course of their lifetimes? For what purposes will they enter the tall skyscrapers? With what obligations and power? And what role is the school system playing in either promoting or breaking the vicious cycles that have so far constructed the problematic relationships of the neighborhood's residents to this metropolis?

The history of El Sereno is not well documented, as Mr. Dueñas discovered when he asked his students to research their community in his summer California History course. His summer school students Brandon and Jonathan spent countless hours looking for information. Their search led them to only a few websites (mostly Wikipedia entries) that displayed a brief outline of their community's history. This left his students wondering why their community had no solid, documented history. These students used what little information they could gather, interviewed a fellow schoolmate, and began to write their own community history. They wrote a paper and created a PowerPoint presentation entitled "Major Problems in El Sereno History." Their research and struggles to find just a basic understanding of their community's history motivated Mr. Dueñas to keep up his search as well. The only historical sources he has been able to find are at the local library, where a longtime librarian in the community has managed to piece together newspaper clippings and a city report to retell the community's history.

Like many other neighborhoods in the North East Los Angeles area, El Sereno is not well known, except among local residents and those from surrounding communities. Its more affluent neighboring communities, like Pasadena and Alhambra, are more recognizable to most people outside of the local area. This neglected part of Los Angeles has a special history, however. It is mostly acknowledged in Chicano History books that mention the area's important role in the student Chicano movement, where Wilson High School students, many of them residents of El Sereno, were key participants in the Chicano Student Blowouts of 1968.

Just as the demographics of its original inhabitants shifted from the Tongva, to Spanish missionaries and colonizers, to Mexican, and then to American ranchers, its more recent inhabitants shifted from settlers of northern European descent in the early 1900s to Italian Americans during the wartime boom of the 1930s and 1940s, to its current, heavily Latino population. Many Mexican American families started living in El Sereno when housing ordinances were changed in 1948 to allow them to live in the community due to the Supreme Court case of *Shelly v. Kraemer* (Casen, 1994). This demographic shift was highlighted when, in 1968, students from El Sereno were the first to walk out of class at Wilson High School because they and three local schools, Roosevelt, Lincoln, and Garfield, had organized to address the educational problems facing Latino/a students in their communities. Wilson jumped the gun and walked out earlier than the other three schools because of discontent over the school administration's handling of a play. This student activism helped change overall conditions for the Latino student in El Sereno, but some discontent persists. For the student and local residents, poverty is still an issue, along with gang violence. In the 1980s and 1990s, there was a height of gang violence in El Sereno, but it has somewhat subsided as happened with many communities all over Los Angeles. All problems aside, residents of El Sereno are very proud of their community, which is visible at local parks, where various generations of El Sereno residents play and watch Little League baseball or football games.

Wilson High School

Woodrow Wilson High School first opened in 1937 in what is now El Sereno Middle School, located on Eastern Avenue. Classes were separated into winter and summer classes and took place in tents and old bungalows. Construction on the first gymnasium began right before World War II and was completed in 1942. The first senior class of 40 students graduated in the winter of 1940. Since opening its doors, the school has had 12 full-time principals. In 1970, Wilson Senior High School moved to its new campus atop a large hill overlooking the city. On a clear day, Catalina Island is visible to the south and Mt. Baldy appears to the north. In 2007, Wilson celebrated its 70th anniversary.

Over the past 5 years, Wilson's faculty has made strategic and dedicated efforts to improve the school. For example, they created thematic Small Learning Communities to offer opportunities for students to study areas of business, law, health sciences, visual and performing arts, transportation and urban issues, and social justice. The school has also participated in a community-wide effort to become an International Baccalaureate (IB) school with the local feeder elementary and middle schools, and adopted school-wide strategies that promote a college-bound mind-set for students. Common planning time for departments and SLCs gives faculty time to work together and continuously pursue and implement professional development to advance the success of all students.

Enrollment at Woodrow Wilson High School

The demographics at Wilson High show the school to be highly segregated ethnically. Even though the state schools host a Latino plurality (at 49%) and the district has a Latino majority at 72%, Wilson High, with more than 90% of its students coming from Latino backgrounds, is primarily a mono-racial school. However, Asian American students are also prominent in school government and other leadership positions. The other ethnic groups are largely invisible on the campus. During the 2008–2009 academic year, Woodrow Wilson Senior High enrolled 2457 students with the following ethnic breakdown: White: 0.4%, African American: 1.7%, Hispanic: 93.6%, Asian American: 3.5%,

Filipino: 0.4%, American Indian: 0.3%, and Multi: 0.4% (Ed-Data, 2011); 22.2% of the students are classified as English Language learners, and 80.5% qualify for free and reduced lunch.

Academic Achievement at Woodrow Wilson High

High school completion rates are reported in many different ways and, for this reason, they are frequently a source of great controversy and debate. For the class of 2009, the COR for Wilson High was 100:42:21 (http://idea.gseis.ucla.edu/educational-opportunity-report/2011/).

The college opportunity ratio data for Wilson High reveals a consistent, yet troubling, pattern with schools across the region. For every 100 students who start high school, only 2 in 5 are around to cross the graduation stage 4 years later. By contrast, at a nearby affluent school less than 10 miles away, 90 of 100 students make it to graduation. Of that original 100 students entering Wilson High with high hopes for their futures, whose families make tremendous sacrifice for these futures, only 21 students will have completed the requirements even to be eligible for admission to the state's universities. That leaves nearly 80 young people out of 100 who leave Wilson High either without a diploma or without much hope of continuing their education. In our increasingly technologically dependent society, what lies ahead for these students? How will they feed their families? How will they pursue their passions? How will they avoid the almost unavoidable cycles of social reproduction? Two clues to the futures are evident in a drive (or long walk) up the hill that leads to the school. One is the constant flow of police cars up and down the street. The second is the literature often strewn across campus from the various branches of the military seeking out new recruits. Apparently, there are many in power who believe Wilson High doesn't have much of a shot of producing a future president of the United States, but instead that many of these students will leave campus to find themselves locked in low-wage labor, in military service, or as long-term guests in the state's fastest growing institutions, its prisons.

The Agents of Change:
Small Learning Community at Wilson High School

In school year 2007–2008, Wilson High School formally organized into SLCs. Teachers and staff devoted a significant amount of time and energy to creating SLCs that reflected the needs and interests of students and staff. Mr. Dueñas and Ms. Garcia were given the Agents of Change (AOC) SLC. The mission of AOC is to graduate academically prepared and socially aware individuals ready to better their world by empowering them to (1) develop a strong sense of identity, (2) get involved in their communities, (3) learn about issues around the world, (4) become advocates for change, and (5) pursue a higher education. The vision is to better the world by (1) promoting identity; (2) encouraging meaningful curriculum; (3) creating partnerships in the business, public, and nonprofit sectors; (4) celebrating students' successes; and (5) providing students with critical thinking skills to succeed in higher education. Over the past few years, teachers in AOC have organized various school activities for its 300 students in grades 9–12. AOC students are diverse in their circumstances and experiences; over the years, this SLC has seen high numbers of students with attendance issues, with time in the juvenile justice system and/or in foster care, being raised by single and non-parent households (i.e., grandparents), and with low achievement levels. Thus, AOC strives to support students by engaging in learning and relationships that address their critical needs and interests. Staff members are encouraged to embed the AOC mission and vision into their curriculum, as well as model the qualities and characteristics of an AOC individual. Over the years, AOC has organized activities such as historical mural paintings, fasting in honor of Cesar Chavez, college and career days, clothes drives, and fundraising for the victims of Japan's earthquake. For the past 2 years, an AOC student council has taken charge to organize events and discussions and to galvanize the students and faculty around critical civic issues.

THE COUNCIL OF YOUTH RESEARCH (1999–2011)

Background

The third space we will examine is a summer program offered to youth throughout the city of Los Angeles. This program, co-founded by Mr. Morrell and his colleague John Rogers of UCLA's Institute for Democracy, Education, and Access (IDEA), has focused on developing youth as researchers and advocates for their own neighborhoods and schools. The project essentially has two goals: (1) to increase the academic literacy and college readiness of youth through learning critical research skills and (2) to increase awareness about inequities in schools through engaging youth as advocates on their own behalf. Each year, approximately 30 students participate in a summer program held at the university where they learn about academic research, design and conduct research projects in their schools and neighborhoods, and present this research in a public forum, generally Los Angeles City Hall. The students write research reports, prepare PowerPoint presentations, and create their own digital videos. There are also after-school and Saturday-school components throughout the academic year that include local presentations, work in their home schools, and participation at national professional conferences such as the American Educational Research Association (AERA) and Digital Media and Learning (DML). The Council of Youth Research, which has been offered annually from 1999–2011, has involved teachers and students from the East LA high schools from its inception. At any given time, about 10 of the 30 students are representing Wilson and Roosevelt high schools. Additionally, Mr. López, Mr. Dueñas, and Ms. Garcia have all taught in the summer program, and Mr. Morrell has directed each of the summer seminars as well as the year-long program since the program's inception.

Program Logistics and Accomplishments

The Council of Youth Research (CYR) has experienced success on both of its major goals. The overwhelming majority of the student participants complete high school and go on to attend major universities throughout the nation. It has also shown the quality of its academic literacy development via participation in this project through other research (Morrell, 2008). The students have been able to reach wide audiences with their research. This includes forums with the U.S. Secretary of Education, the mayor of Sacramento, the mayor of Los Angeles, state and federal legislators and their staff members, superintendents, principals, classroom teachers, parents, fellow students, members of the media, and educational researchers. The Youth Council has enjoyed media coverage by outlets including CNN, local newspapers, radio stations, and Internet blogs. The Youth Council students also have their own Internet presence via their YouTube page, their Twitter and Facebook pages, and their links via the UCLA Institute for Democracy, Education, and Access website.

STUDYING YOUTH MEDIA PRODUCTION
IN CLASSROOMS AND COMMUNITIES

In this section, we will discuss our approach to researching media literacy development across these programs, but it seems premature to jump to mechanisms for data collection and analysis without stopping for at least a moment to think about how our theories of knowledge (epistemologies) inform how we choose to ask questions, how we choose to collect information that will help us to answer those questions, and how we make sense of the information that we collect. Our epistemological orientation begins with the proposition that all knowledge is constructed by certain individuals and organizations to serve social purposes. While intentions are often good and the knowledge produced may make life better or easier or more coherent, sometimes knowledge is created that is harmful to people. If that is the case, particularly when we are working with or on behalf of people who have been negatively affected by existing regimes of truth (Foucault, 1972), then we have to make certain considerations when adding information to the cultural reservoir:

1. How is the current power-knowledge regime flawed? If we begin with the proposition that all knowledge is interested knowledge, we must understand that it is flawed. We need to be willing to look at the historical contexts of the knowledge produced and understand how its social construction is a product of power hierarchies and positioning. This isn't necessarily bad as long as it is transparent. But we should be skeptical about all sources of knowledge, and we should also feel comfortable overriding previous social truths once we have access to better or more distanced information. For instance, while we hold on to Thomas Jefferson's ideas about democracy, we wouldn't want to hold on to his ideas about African Americans because they are crafted in a context where Africans were slaves in Jefferson's possession.
2. Who gets to say what is so? Operating from a critical epistemological framework, we would want to know who has voice and who is silenced. Who gets to participate in the process of knowledge production? We should want to hear from those who have been ill affected by the current reality. Critical epistemologies find multiple sites of entry

for those who have been voiceless, whether that is through collaborative research or through honoring voice and narratives in data collection and analysis.

3. Why do we collect the information that we do? The purpose of work is to understand and ultimately intervene in the world around us. We know what we know and we have certain responsibilities to act upon what we know, especially if that information can be used to transform existing realities. Paulo Freire (1970) pronounced that to name a word is simultaneously to act upon the world. Knowing is participating and doing at the same time. There is not the pause or gap where it is possible to have information and not to act upon that information or not to be changed by that information. We are, after all, products of what we know and what we have done and will do. This has tremendous implications for researchers, who have traditionally been able to distance themselves from the work they have done, as if it were possible to create knowledge and then not be responsible for that knowledge created. That cannot be true; research changes and compels first and foremost the researcher him- or herself.

CRITICAL ETHNOGRAPHY

Each of us is a participant in this drama that we attempt to recount. But we do not see this as a detriment to the work that we do. In fact, it is indispensable to the work. We draw upon the ethnographic tradition that dates back to the early 20th century and cultural anthropologists such as Margaret Mead, Bronislaw Malinowski, and Franz Boas who engaged in longitudinal studies of local cultural practices. Geertz (1983) describes "ethnography" as a process of unpacking how people see themselves in the world through engaging in the process of thick description of events that hold symbolic importance to them. In its best light, ethnography has been an additive perspective on cultural practice. Anthropologists and others who use ethnographic tools have been able to outline the logic of cultural practice, and they have been able to demonstrate the complex functioning of all cultures, particularly those that have been misinterpreted or misunderstood.

This also creates problems, when the ethnographer, usually an outsider, is the one who is doing the interpreting. Often, the ethnographer's "eyes" are colored by race, class, and privilege, and the voices of those being studied are frequently muted in this process. These hierarchies problematize the accuracy of the representations of the "other" in classic ethnography. The guise of objectivity also falls under increased scrutiny as we unpack the relationship among ideology, positionality, and the work of the ethnographer. While this is not only an issue with ethnographers, the discipline has, admirably, engaged in public self-reflection on this issue. Scholars such as Norm Denzin (1994) have discussed this crisis of representation and asked for narratives that are more multi-voiced. This has been echoed in the work of postcolonial scholars such as Gayatri Spivak who asks in a famous essay "Can the Subaltern Speak?" (1988).

It is out of this tradition that critical ethnography emerges. It is still ethnography in the sense that the work sets out to unpack cultural life in neighborhoods, families, subcultures, and schools. It is critical in the sense that it feigns no objectivity; the work is dedicated to the proposition of uncovering issues of power, oppression, and resistance in historically marginalized communities. Second, critical ethnographies, whenever possible, privilege the first-person narrative and the voice of those who are implicated in the struggle. Third, the ethnographer does not exist outside of the practice; he/she is a participant in and with those who are not only the objects of study, but also co-subjects in the creation of the story of cultural production (Kincheloe & McLaren, 1998). As ethnographers in the critical tradition, we have lived as educators in these schools and projects for more than a decade; we have advocated with and on behalf of the students and schools; we have, whenever possible, referenced the work and the voices of the students; and we have tried to situate this practice within the larger project of social justice and educational transformation without qualms.

PARTICIPATORY ACTION RESEARCH

In addition to wearing the hats of critical ethnographers who are trying to understand these various cultural practices of Roosevelt, Wilson, and the CYR, we are also educators actively involved in the design, implementation, and study of curricular interventions that, among others, focus on the inclusion of media. To situate this second aspect of our study, we draw on the growing methodological approach known as *participatory action research*. Participatory action research is unique from many other prevalent methodologies in education studies and the social sciences in its "who," its "how," and its "why" (Morrell, 2008). With respect to the "who" of action research, it is generally research conducted with or by those populations most involved with the issue to be studied—in this case, teachers and students. We argue that the populations that are most affected by educational policies should be more centrally involved in knowledge production in our field. Only when we have more teachers involved in documenting life in their classrooms will we have the information we need to make better policy decisions about rigorous and relevant curricula and instruction across the disciplines.

With respect to the "how," action research is collaborative in nature. Here, we have a 4-person research team of K–12 and university educators as well as a group of 20 high school students involved in research, and students in the focal classrooms are also conducting their own research. It is this collaborative and participatory nature of the research, we argue, that allows us to tell an intimate, multi-vocal, and more humane account of life in these classrooms and community projects. Nor do we feel that any of the adjectives mentioned in the previous sentence take away from the rigor, the quality, and the veracity of these accounts. Rather, we feel that each augments the possibilities for representing this work in powerful and unique ways.

Finally, we distinguish action research by its "why." The participatory action research tradition has been focused on collecting and analyzing data and disseminating scholarly information for the purpose of social transformation and justice. We feel that participatory action research will play an integral role in the future of educational inquiry because of its emphasis on change and its incorporation of previously muted voices from the research conversation.

LITERACY, CONSCIENTIZATION, AND MEDIA PRODUCTION

In our work with youth, we looked for outcomes across three major domains: literacy, conscientization, and media production. For the first, we draw upon the work of ethnography of communication and, in particular, the New Literacy Studies of Brian Street, Shirley Bryce

Heath, Marc Lamont Hill, Maisha Winn, and Valerie Kinloch. For the development of conscientization, we turn to the critical pedagogical scholarship of Paulo Freire, Donaldo Macedo, Shirley Steinberg, Joe Kincheloe, and bell hooks and the work on critical language awareness done by such scholars as Norm Fairclough and H. Samy Alim. Finally, for media production, we have looked to exciting new work in semiotics and visual sociology, and we have drawn on scholars such as Gunther Kress.

New literacy scholars such as Street (1984), Heath (1982), Hill (2009), Kinloch (2010), and Barton and Hamilton (2000) moved the field forward both conceptually and methodologically. Conceptually, they have helped us to understand that literacies are multiple, culturally situated, and connected to hierarchies of power. This new conception of literacies helped us to move from defining certain groups as "illiterate" to working to understand how each culture uses language and literacy in its everyday practices. This led to the methodological advances through the many ethnographies of literacy, where researchers went into communities to document the powerful uses of literacy in out-of-school settings. Of particular value are the contributions of Shirley Bryce Heath (1982) and David Barton and Mary Hamilton (2000), who identified the literacy event as a key coding scheme. We follow this example in documenting the literacy events of the youth as they are involved in the activity of media production.

In his breakthrough work *Pedagogy of the Oppressed*, Paulo Freire (1970) discussed the role of a problem-posing education in leading to the conscientization of historically marginalized populations. For Freire, this person, who worked toward a critical consciousness, is able to read the word and the world and act upon that world in informed and empowered ways. Others have talked about this connection between literacy and agency, such as Frederick Douglass (1845) who, in his first autobiography, discusses the role that becoming critically literate played in his view of slavery, himself, and the possibilities for freedom. bell hooks (1994) discusses the role of critical consciousness in the process of self-actualization, and Carter G. Woodson, in *Miseducation of the Negro* (1972), enforces the importance of re-educating ourselves out of habits of servitude and acquiescence. Each of these authors describes a transformational experience that is manifest through a different relationship to knowledge and to power. As researchers, we have attempted to codify this conscientization through students' critical language awareness (Fairclough, 1989; Alim, 2006) and their civic engagement. With respect to the critical language awareness, we paid special attention to places where youth were offering critical explanations for inequity and where they used their literacy skills to speak the truth to power. We also documented instances where young people have drawn on these language and literacy skills to work for social change.

How do we systematically codify and represent visual still and moving images in social science research? How does the visual differ from our representations of other forms of print text such as novels, poems, and nonfiction? If we are going to meaningfully incorporate media consumption into our literacy instruction across the humanities, we must also account for the image, for the semiotic, and we must acknowledge multiple modes of production. As literacy educators and teachers of English and social studies, we realized that we needed a new set of codes to understand the nature of the youth media production in our classroom and community projects. We needed to understand the processes of production—the production as a sociocultural activity—and we needed to understand the quality of the production and possibly its social/societal impact. Both semiotic analysis and visual sociology give us systematic tools and languages to understand and represent visual images in social science research. Visual sociology is a field that attempts to study visual images produced as part of culture. Art, photographs, film, video, fonts, advertisements, computer icons, landscape, architecture, machines, fashion, makeup, hair style, facial expressions, tattoos, and so on, are parts of the complex visual communication system produced by members of societies.

To help us understand the relationship between our work and the development of literacy, conscientization, and powerful media production, we consulted the following forms of data: curricular materials (lesson plans, activities, unit plans, etc.); samples of student media production; digital video documentaries, PowerPoint presentations, t-shirts, posters, newsletters, and so on; samples of other student work; ethnographic field notes of classroom life; conversations with students about their work; and conversations among teachers about our practice.

4 Critical Media Pedagogy in Ms. Garcia's Class

I have worked with urban youth and adults in the Boston and Los Angeles school districts over the past 13 years. My earliest teaching experiences were shaped by my role as an undergraduate serving as an after-school coordinator and mentor in Los Angeles Unified School District (LAUSD). I learned the importance of establishing relationships with parents and teachers to support the preparation of first-generation college-bound students. I continued mentoring, tutoring, and teaching youth in the Boston Public Schools (BPS) as a student at Harvard's Graduate School of Education. At Harvard, I learned the fundamentals of academic research by studying issues of school climate and the engagement level of students and parents in BPS. As the program associate for the Boston Plan for Excellence, I worked locally and nationally with district and school administrators, teachers, funders, evaluators, and community members to make changes in instruction and form small learning communities. I trained BPS high school students as action researchers to engage their voice in the district's improvement efforts by working collaboratively with adults. When I returned to California, I began working with UCLA's Institute for Democracy, Education, and Access as a lead teacher for their Council of Youth Research. In this role, I continued to support students in their efforts to research issues facing their schools and the larger community of LA. These experiences taught me the importance of providing students with a strong curriculum—one that would allow me to develop relationships with them, but also hold them to high standards and expectations.

    I am currently a doctoral student writing my dissertation. My study will capture the literacy and schooling narratives of incarcerated Latino youth; the idea of this study comes directly from my teaching experiences. As I write about this work, the faces of the many students I've had over the years continually resurface in my mind. The faces of students who graduated and went on to college, but also the faces of students who dropped out too soon or got caught up in the juvenile and even adult correctional systems. The latter are faces of mostly Latino males. These students who didn't make it are the ones that hurt the most because I know they had potential. While they left too soon, I know they could have produced. I saw it with my own eyes, in my own classroom—and their peers saw it, too. And I know from their stories written in my classroom, they were ignored and faced many negative schooling experiences throughout their education. For this, I do what I do for my students. I teach these units and with this pedagogy because it is humanizing and empowering for students. I give all my students a voice; a place to write, read, and think; and a nurturing and supportive environment. And in the end, even the most struggling student produces; they all produce.

—Veronica Garcia

BECOMING CRITICAL

Ms. Garcia wants students to understand that learning is reflective. Challenging mainstream or long-held beliefs about issues or topics is critical to making their own meaning of these ideas. Students should feel comfortable bringing their experiences outside of school, such as home, community/neighborhood, family, friends, and observations into the classroom environment. This idea builds on much of the learning theory espoused by such scholars as John Dewey (1900), Paulo Freire (1970), and Gloria Ladson-Billings (1994), who suggest that situating learning in the everyday lives of youth and allowing them to participate meaningfully in their social world increases academic literacy development, relevance, motivation, cultural competence, and civic engagement.

Becoming Experts and Intellectuals

Many scholars have talked about students having a negative (or nonexistent) image of themselves as smart or talented (Fine, 1991; Ladson-Billings, 1994). These negative identities, often fueled by educational institutions, lead to low academic self-concept, a lack of motivation, and ultimately low academic performance or even drop-out (Oakes, 1985; Valenzuela, 1999). To combat these negative academic identities, Ms. Garcia wants her students to feel confident in their abilities no matter their background or previously held stereotypes or beliefs about them in schools. By the time students get to high school, they have been shaped by 9 years of schooling. Those teachers and classrooms do not always support a positive academic self-concept for students. In her attempts to provide a culturally relevant pedagogy that builds academic self-concept, Ms. Garcia relies on students to help her understand new ideas or ways of thinking about topics they study together. Students bring prior knowledge to the classroom, and it must be acknowledged and validated. Students come with experiences from their former schools, families, peers, communities, and popular culture that must be recognized as true knowledge of subjects they study in the classroom. For example, before starting a unit, Ms. Garcia asks students what they already know about the subject, which can help other students become familiar with the information. Teachers often refer to this in the form of a "KWL" chart. The "K" represents what students already know about the topic, the "W" is for what students want to know about the topic, and the "L" represents what students have learned at the end of the unit.

Developing Critical Academic Literacies (Reading, Writing, Critical Thinking, Analysis)

In Ms. Garcia's English classes, her goal is that students will leave the classroom having gained the core and essential skills necessary to advance to the next grade level. The California English Language Arts Standards for students in grade 9 and 10 have similar genres and skills. The standards cover three key areas: *Reading, Writing,* and *Written and Oral English Language Conventions.* Within these areas, students cover genres such as narrative, persuasion, exposition, and literary response and analysis. These genres form the core of the four units agreed upon and covered by the English department. In addition, the standards call for students to learn the mechanics of writing and public speaking, but also how to produce various texts that are of high quality. All of Ms. Garcia's lessons are both critical and standards-based. Students read, write, and think in a critical manner throughout the year. They are challenged with ideas and questions that allow them to examine difficult topics that mimic a college setting with high academic expectations. In order for students to reach academic achievement and critical consciousness, her classroom incorporates the following components.

Emphasis on "critical." All the students' writing assignments are labeled as "CRITICAL." For example, students write a Critical Literacy Narrative, a Critical Life Poem, and a Critical Persuasive Essay. The classroom is a space for students to explore deep social issues, many of which influence students in their school and community. By re-framing assignments and connecting them to kids' everyday lives, students are given a voice and can express their thoughts.

Use of popular culture. Lessons and curricula include resources from the Internet, music, images, television, and video/film from popular culture. These materials allow students to make connections between the traditional curriculum and information that relates to their own participation in youth cultures.

Focus on cultural relevance. The curriculum is centered on students' lives and environments, such as family, community, and school. Students draw upon their own knowledge and culture as they study different topics. Issues of race, ethnicity, language, and other cultural concepts are explored as students are introduced to and complete the units.

Rigorous, quality student products. Students are expected and supported to complete challenging work assignments, whether oral or written. Students are held to a college-level standard. At times, adults from the school or other educational and community organizations are invited to attend presentations that validate students as intellectuals.

With these key elements in mind, Ms. Garcia crafted several classroom units that allow students to successfully meet the standards, develop critical perspectives, and engage in critical media literacy curriculum. For each of the following examples, we describe how the unit was developed, discuss the process for producing student work, provide student work samples, and offer reflection on the unit's outcome.

UNIT: A DAY IN MY LIFE AND CRITICAL LITERACY NARRATIVE

In Ms. Garcia's first year of teaching, she struggled to find a way to engage her 9th-graders in a double-block, 2-hour English course. Students had been placed in the Studio Course (which no longer exists) because their reading scores were at a 4th to 6th-grade reading level. The class was predominantly male, and many of them had had negative experiences in school and years of low achievement. Ms. Garcia sought help from Mr. Morrell for an engaging and challenging writing assignment—a way for students to share more about themselves in a safe space. Thus, "A Day in My Life" was adapted from an assignment that the students in the UCLA Council of Youth Research had done in one of the summer seminars. The students described a day in their lives using many details, incorporating critical thinking about these experiences and conditions they faced from morning until night. At first, the students focused on creating the written essay, but over time they also incorporated visual elements, which included digital photographs and ultimately a digital story with images and music that they edited on Microsoft Moviemaker. The assignment was a huge success. During the winter, Ms. Garcia's students traveled to UCLA to share their written and digital stories with college students and faculty. During the spring, the *Learning Power* online news source at UCLA's Institute for Democracy, Education, and Access published three stories in its online newsletter (http://learningpower.gseis.ucla.edu/articles_3/story1.html) featuring the work of these 9th-grade students. Often, teachers make assumptions about students and what they are *not* doing, but this assignment was an eye-opening opportunity for Ms. Garcia to better understand what her students go through on a daily basis. She wanted to make the classroom an intellectual, culturally relevant, and productive space, and she did not understand why the students were not responding. This assignment allowed her to discover how students were being treated and the kinds of expectations other teachers had for them, most of which were counterproductive to the high expectations she carried in the class.

It is very important for Ms. Garcia to know the kinds of schooling experiences her students have had in their previous years before they go through her class. The "Day in My Life" assignment pushed her to consider another assignment that would be similar and could be done early on in the school year to tap into students' prior schooling experiences. In those first days of school, students fill out a questionnaire and discuss reading and writing. The students' responses indicated that many of them come to class never having written a full essay and don't feel confident about writing. So, as an extension of "A Day in My Life," Ms. Garcia created the Critical Literacy Narrative unit as a way for students to share about their lives as readers and writers, but also begin the school year in a powerful way.

In this assignment, students must share their elementary and middle school years' experiences (both positive and negative) and end with final thoughts about how to start their high school careers. It is important to know how teachers and peers treated students in their previous schools. The specific assignments or powerful moments students write about are significant to these narratives so that Ms. Garcia may replicate those positive experiences, but the events they share about negative instances are just as important. This assignment is the first step in creating a community in the classroom as well because, through the process of writing, students are asked to work with one another. It is a powerful resource for students to have a first paper they can feel proud of and that is all about them. This is how the school year begins.

Students go through an intense writing process to produce their Critical Literacy Narratives. Because it is the beginning of the year, this assignment takes time to build. Students must not only craft a long story about their lives, but also follow specific writing rules that must be learned right away. There is a lot of revising as well, which prolongs the unit. Ms. Garcia extends the time for the unit as long as necessary so that students have a strong, well-written paper they can use and refer to over the course of the year. To get students thinking about the topic of their lives, students are given warm-up questions such as the following: What are your thoughts about school in general? How do adults perceive students based on your experiences? Describe the kind of student you are. What are you like as a reader/writer? How do you study? How did you learn to be the kind of student you are? How do you feel about school? What is the purpose of education? Are you (or have you) been receiving the kind of education you deserve? Students answer these questions in their own writing journals during the first few days of school. As a class, they take notes and chart responses publicly around the room. This allows students to see their shared connections and stories. These questions are accessible to all students and allow everyone to participate. In addition, their responses to these prompts can be used for parts of their paper.

As the class discusses critical questions that make up the paper, Ms. Garcia also weaves in music and other literary sources into the lessons. Students use a quote from a music artist or other educational philosopher they are introduced to (or from their own music collection) in their paper. Students listen to music and relate deeply to artists from different genres, so allowing them to use music in their writing validates their personal interests and creativity. The hip hop music they analyze has lyrics that describe the power of youth (and people in general) to educate themselves and fight against issues such as oppression, racism, and overall discrimination. In these songs, the artists share their views, experiences, and ideas about situations that happened to them, many of which are shared by the students themselves, including poverty, racism, struggling parents, and relationships. In addition to music, students also read excerpts from authors who struggled in their childhood or with their own literacy development. Students always have their own copy of the song or reading, a highlighter, and pen/pencil. The text is also available on the LCD projector to provide a visual when the class annotates the lines together. Throughout the analysis of text, Ms. Garcia works in sync with the students to model how to break down lines and phrases of the lyrics or reading and make notes on the paper. After students break down the text in "chunks" for meaning, they discuss tone, mood, theme, connotation, and diction. Students become familiar with these terms right away and are able to use them throughout the year in other units as well as district and state assessments. Usually, students draw out themes about the importance of education and self-confidence and identify the message that everyone can change for the better, so it is important never to stop trying.

After they explore examples from popular music, students read excerpts from *Building Academic Literacy: An Anthology for Reading Apprenticeship* by Audrey Fielding and Ruth Schoenbach (2003), which contains short stories by authors from all over the world, such as Luis Rodriguez, Gary Soto, or Greg Sarris, who struggled to read, write, or even see themselves as intellectuals. Students make connections to the authors' stories and again find common themes between the authors and music artists. At the end of the unit, students have at least four or five different texts and songs that are annotated with ideas about the meaning and charted with literary terms. Their student work looks very similar to how college and graduate students make meaning from their own readings and take notes. The music and stories also challenge the students' thinking about social issues that not only pertain to them, but also come from many different sources. Students learn to ask higher-level questions and find similarities and differences with each other early on in the year.

Modeling the desired outcome—essay—of this unit has been key to the high quality and production of student work. Throughout the entire process, Ms. Garcia makes sure that there are writing samples for students to draw upon and use if necessary. Students read Ms. Garcia's narrative and other sample narratives by former students. This sharing of previously written stories helps students understand what the paper is about and how to write their own. It is important for students to build confidence in their writing abilities as they write stories.

Having strong samples on hand allows everyone to see the end product. Ms. Garcia also prints out sample introductions, thesis statements, topic sentences, and transition sentences for students to have as they write. There is a list of "baby words" that students cannot use in their writing, which encourages the use of the thesaurus and builds higher vocabulary. Students also learn the structure of a well-written essay: introduction, body paragraphs, and closing. Each student chooses an artist or author to quote in his or her paper and must analyze the text and share how it applies to his or her own educational journey. This paper goes through at least three drafts.

Sample Excerpts

NOTE: The students' excerpts were kept as original writings and may contain some errors.

Excerpt 1

I knew that I had to get ready for high school, so I also got serious about my work. During this time I feel that I relate to the author Paulo Freire because he explains that to study or read can be a difficult process and might take time, but the reward is much greater. These are ideas I live by. In "First Letter" (Chapter in: Teachers as Cultural Workers: Letters to Those Who Dare Teach), *Paulo Freire (1998) says, "If I am really studying, seriously reading, I cannot go past a page if I cannot grasp its significance clearly" (pg. 18). What I think this quote means is no matter how much you study or read, you cannot move on with understanding the importance in it first. This quote matters to my story because I have been trying my hardest in school and life. If I don't understand something at first, such as in school or football, I can't move on. I told myself to be prepared for what I have coming because for the next four years, I'm thinking about this quote*

—Salvador

Excerpt 2

My teenage years are completely different from elementary school years. In middle school I tried to be more of a gangster/screw-up than a student. I wanted to be the cholo like the people that sang rap and were rich and famous. I wanted to be like them. That's why it was such a problem. I was in what is called a crew, which is for future gangsters. I didn't care about reading and lost my interest in school. Maybe because I didn't receive any help from my teachers or I felt that they just didn't care. I had a teacher that once told me that he didn't think I was going to reach my goals of becoming a lawyer. One of the artists I related to was NAS because he reminds us that just because we are living in the "ghetto" doesn't mean we can't achieve. NAS emphasizes reaching goals no matter what. According to NAS in the song "I Can" he tells us, "You think life's all about smoking weed and ice. You don't want to be my age and not can't read and write." This means that life isn't worth the drugs and gangs, there's more to life than that. If you want to succeed, you better shape up and learn how to read and write. We must stop fighting with our fists and fight with our pens. This quote talks about my middle school years.

—Francisco

Excerpt 3

Ms. Butler didn't give up on me and as time passed, I was less embarrassed to read in class.... That same year my mom signed me up for LA's Best. She wanted me to get some extra help since my English wasn't that perfect and my third grade teacher wouldn't offer as much help as Ms. Butler offered. I hated LA's Best because there I met a lot people that didn't like me. I don't know why. What I hated the most was that people in my group wouldn't call me by my name, they would say, "Hey girl," sometimes even "Spanish girl."... It made me feel friendless and isolated from everybody else, I felt as if I didn't belong and as if I was being discriminated... they thought they were better than me just because their English was very well. I hated that year... let's just say third grade was my worst year of elementary.

—Elisa

The narrative assignment over the past 3 years has allowed Ms. Garcia to better understand her students and create a classroom environment that is welcoming to all. It provides insights into unjust situations and encounters the students have experienced with other adults in their young lives. This unit is a critical experience for students because many of them have never taken the opportunity to think about their school history. For the previous 8 years, students went to school, some learning, but many just going through the motions of education. The students' excerpts show just how alienated they feel. For example, Jesus's excerpt highlights peer pressures at a young age—middle school—and how he is drawn to negative influences. At the time, Jesus didn't care about anything else and did not think his teachers would care either. Yet, in the rapper NAS's song, Jesus is able to reflect on just a few lines to think critically about his future. He knows that the past will not be the judge of his future. Elisa's story reminds educators about the immigrant experience that so many students face in public schools and the need for caring and supportive school environments. Fortunately, Elisa had a teacher who recognized her intellect and encouraged her to seek more learning, yet Elisa was ridiculed by her peers for not knowing English in that tutoring environment.

The essay is also helpful for showing how each student writes and the strengths and challenges facing their literacy development. The assignment also provides information about the kinds of music, literature, and people students are drawn to as they look for connections with others. For students, the narrative becomes a sharing process where they learn about common experiences, teachers, schools, cities, and other locations. Students also build confidence in their ability to write an academically strong paper in the first month or two of school. They learn how to use and break down quotes and make meaning from these words to apply to their own stories. Next, students are exposed to ideas about how to define quality. Their narratives aren't just about telling a story, but about thinking critically about education for marginalized youth. They are asked to critique situations that were both positive and negative and think about the consequences of those experiences on their learning.

The critical literacy narrative unit sets the tone for the kind of learning environment Ms. Garcia wants for her students: rigorous, challenging, supportive, and community oriented. It is very easy for teachers and administrators to push a less personalized unit on students from the start without taking the time to get to know their backgrounds. Teachers will struggle greatly if they don't take time to work with students and validate their prior knowledge and experiences. It is important to know the reasons students may be turned off (or love) learning. Because this unit is done at the start of the year, it can become complicated and "messy" for teachers, and they may be discouraged about attempting the unit. At times, it has felt too long because students' writing skills are developing and they need to work at a slow pace. However, in order for students to learn how to write well and with a passion, this process must be completed. This assignment is organized so that every student can share about his/her life. Students are allowed to focus on one particular incident in their schooling if they are too overwhelmed to write about their entire childhood from elementary to middle school. Their typed narratives are placed in their binders, and students can refer to them all year.

Having music as part of the unit acknowledges the different ways that students can learn. Most students listen to music on a daily basis and already understand how to interpret meaning in the songs they like or relate to. This unit helps them to break down meaning in the "standards-based" way and shows that music can be a part of student learning. Over the past 2 years, Ms. Garcia has also tried to align the prompt, questions, and purpose of the overall assignment to the theme of her Small Learning Community (SLC), which is geared toward social justice and community engagement.

UNIT: ORAL HISTORY AND LITERARY RESPONSE

In spring 2008, the National Endowment for the Arts selected *Bless Me, Ultima* by Rodolfo Anaya as the book of choice for the annual Big Read celebration. Ms. Garcia was in touch with the librarian in City Terrace, a local neighborhood, over the school year and she was asked to participate in reading this book with her students. The library provides various school and summer services to Wilson High School students and the surrounding community. The librarian delivered more than 40 brand-new paperback copies of the novel, CDs containing an interview with the author, posters, and bookmarks for students. In addition, the Wilson High School librarian also sponsored and encouraged students to read this book. Ms. Garcia wanted students to take a deeper approach to reading this text, which focused on the childhood of a young man named Antonio, who is on a journey to learn about his past and family history, but also to seek out his destiny. Many of the students had never spoken to their family members about their cultural or educational experiences. Ms. Garcia hoped the book unit would allow students not only to dig into their own family history, but also to access multiple literacy modes of learning: reading, writing, oral communication, PowerPoint development, public-speaking/ presentation skills, and use of media.

Students studied the background of the author and the relevant time and place before reading the book. They did a gallery walk, where students silently travel the classroom perusing images of New Mexico and Latinos at that time. Many of the images were those captured from the book. Due to the close of the school year, the class was only able to read the first five chapters. Students read enough of the book to take in the main idea of the story—Antonio was discovering the roots and foundation of his family and pursuing his future. Antonio's path was one that took him on a journey into his history, culture, traditions, family, and education. He was in search of his destiny and that idea was what Ms. Garcia wanted students to discover for themselves—as the saying goes, "You won't know where you're going unless you know where you came from." As students read, they were required to take notes, keep reading logs, and do small assignments to show comprehension of the book. Shortly after beginning to read, students began preparing for family oral history interviews. Ms. Garcia gave students a handout with ten questions; each set of questions was for their interview with two family members. Their interviews had to be recorded using Cornell Notes, where students divide their notes page in half, the left side for key ideas and questions and the right side devoted to detailed notes. Students could ask for additional information if they wanted or could revise the questions given to them. Using their notes, students had to write and type up an oral history paper, which for most students was at least four pages long. The paper was divided up into the following sections: Introduction, Family Interviews, *Bless Me Ultima* Analysis, and Conclusion. The students' interviews served as the outline for their paper, making it easy for them to complete a full write-up of their family stories. Their papers had to include at least two actual quotes from their family members (one per person). In addition, students were required to create a PowerPoint presentation of their family interviews to present to the class and other invited guests. Ms. Garcia asked them to be specific about what they learned about their past and how this knowledge would inform their future goals, career, and choices.

The PowerPoint slides had to be succinct and not too wordy. Students had to make sure that their slides were organized and had appropriate headings to make the presentation "pleasing to the eye." To help the students complete the task and set up a high expectation for the project, Ms. Garcia modeled each assignment—her own PowerPoint, essay, and interview write-up of her mother and paternal grandmother. Students presented their PowerPoint slides first to their classmates and invited guests from our school. Students had to come dressed professionally, and the formal atmosphere increased the level of expectation for everyone.

The students' work was powerful throughout the unit. Many of the students had never sat down and talked with their family members about their lives and experiences in school, culture, or family history. Throughout the unit, students helped each other with their PowerPoint slides and shared their computer skills and knowledge.

This unit was grounded in critical pedagogy for several reasons. First, students were able to learn and reflect on their own family histories, a process the majority of them had never engaged in. This provided a more appreciative perspective for the sacrifices their parents and relatives made—either in the United States or another country. The students learned information or stories about how their parents or family members experienced life or schooling. Some of the family members had experienced issues of racism, lack of support, and detachment from the school and/or curriculum throughout their education. In this learning process, students were able to have a critical conversation about life and lessons learned from the adults they regarded as important in their lives. As a result, students felt empowered to think about their futures more critically. They wanted to be the first in their families to attend college, graduate, and pursue specific careers. Importantly, the students also considered staying away from negative influences that had affected their family members. This project helped students think more deeply about their own history, much like the journey Antonio took in *Bless Me Ultima*, and come to critical conclusions about the culture, traditions, and sacrifices in their own families.

Students don't always get the opportunity to dialogue with one another about commonalities in their families. In this unit, students found many instances of sharing the same family history, culture, or education experience. It created a stronger sense of unity within the class and relationships between and among students that were not evident before.

The unit also provided students opportunities to develop multiple academic and media literacies. Students were reading, writing, using media in their PowerPoint slides, and gaining strategies for using computer programs and the Internet. The PowerPoint presentations took about 5 days to complete, which is quite fast for 9th-graders. However, many students were already familiar with how to use the Internet and PowerPoint. The level of imagery and media sources students used to incorporate pictures into their PowerPoint slides was quite amazing. Even real pictures from actual family members or cultural artifacts were so easily produced. For example, one student took a picture of a family necklace for her artifact slide. The picture looked as though it had been taken professionally, yet all she had done was put the necklace on a pillow and photograph it herself.

This unit held students to high expectations, and each completed a quality assignment not just alone, but with help and support from their peers. It incorporated reading, writing, and presentation components—all of which were standards based. The presence of adults helped to increase the sense that the students' work was important and worthy of an audience. An improvement to the unit would be to record the presentations to build a media archive of the students' work. Students also could be given more ownership to generate the types of questions they want to ask their family members.

Sample Reflections

Interviewing my parents and learning what they taught me has been a very rewarding experience. I've learned how important my parents' traditions are, and how much they mean to them. I know never to forget where I come from or my culture. I've also learned how important it is to always do my best in school. They have worked hard to provide for our family and all they would want in return is for their children to be educated. To me, my education is very important because I want to go far in life, and make my parents proud.

—Jessica

I learned that I am supposed to do the following: accomplish my goals, follow my dreams and not give up, take advantage of Education, graduate on stage and go to college. I will do this by keeping up my grades doing good in school, getting involved, and, setting goals & believing in myself.

—Vanessa

In education, I will strive to graduate high school and go to college, earn a Bachelor's Degree, and work as a Video Game Developer. I will stay away from drugs and people affiliated with them. I won't fall into temptation.

—Ricardo

I learned to appreciate my life and what my parents have sacrificed to let me live a life with so many choices. I will do something better with my life and move forward so that I would not have the life that they have lived. I will go to college and graduate with a degree in aircraft engineering.

—Joseph

UNIT: CRITICAL POETRY

After years of work with youth, Ms. Garcia knows that many of her students are already writers when they come to class. She has found that they write poetry, songs, or stories on their own. Teachers and educators often don't realize or tap into those skills and experiences, thinking instead that students are ill equipped for writing and literacy. The poetry unit allows students to express their creativity, have a voice on issues that matter to them, and share their words with one another. As a teacher, Ms. Garcia realizes the importance of allowing students to draw from their favorite poets, artists, and writers in this unit. She has used this unit for 5 years with her students.

The unit is called "critical" poetry to encourage students to engage with ideas about how poets and artists share their views about important issues facing society. There are always mixed feelings about poetry at the beginning of the unit—some students (mostly girls) are very excited, and the boys generally express dislike. Students who are not interested in poetry say that it's "boring." Mostly, students feel this way because they haven't experienced poetry as fun or rewarding. They have never had the opportunity to write their own poems in a way that made sense to them.

Ms. Garcia introduces students to the unit with an overview of what they will accomplish. Sample poems and artwork by former students and Ms. Garcia are shown to give the students an idea of what is possible. The class begins with a song, usually hip hop, that incorporates a message about education. For example, Ms. Garcia has used both "I Can" by NAS and "The Message" by Grandmaster Flash. As a class, students break the lyrics into "chunks" and discuss literary terms associated with poetry, such as mood, tone, imagery, and symbolism. Students practice breaking down the lyrics and stanzas and eventually come up with themes. Students then move on to traditional and well-known poems and go through the same process of analysis. Ms. Garcia also uses parts of the book *Hip Hop Poetry and the Classics* (Sitomer & Cirelli, 2004) because it also pairs traditional poems with hip hop music to exemplify literary terms. Once students go through the song analysis process and recognize key poetry terms, they begin writing their own poetry. They start with smaller poems, like love, mood, and personification poems. Finally, they move on to writing more intense issue and life poems. Students spend several weeks writing and revising their poems. During the last week of the unit, students prepare to present; they choose two poems they want to share with the class. Last year, students were shown a poetry slam on YouTube to get an idea of how to present and enhance the presentation of their own poems.

Student Examples

The quality and quantity of work students produce at the end of a 5-week period is quite amazing. Students who expressed dislike or lack of interest in poetry actually end up sharing a great deal about their lives, feelings, and experiences. While students may struggle with the other poems, everyone completes the Critical Life Poem. Additionally, each year, one or two students get emotional during their presentations to the class. These are even students who were very shy to present but, by the time presentations come, allow themselves to express emotions. All the students are very supportive of one another. One year, a student with cerebral palsy and who is in a wheelchair presented her Critical Life Poem. Her poem expressed thoughts of sadness about why she was chosen for this condition and wished that she could play with other students. This student is a wonderful young lady and, despite her physical limitations, has managed to stay positive and hopeful about her life. At the end of her presentation, the students were in tears and truly gained an appreciation for students with disabilities. They

Teen Pregnancy (Critical Life Poem)

Teen Pregnancy by Vanessa Gavia

You find a guy you truly like
Never do you imagine life without him.
Your world spins as he tells you how
    much he loves you.
You do whatever he says, feeling no
    regrets as he lies upon you.
A month passes by and you find out
    you're carrying another life.
You break down on the bathroom floor
    because you're scared what you're
    parents might say.
Who could blame you?
I would too if I was 14 and didn't know
    what to do!
Your first approach is the guy you love
    the most.
Confident because he said, "I'll never
    leave you when you need me the
    most."
You find comfort as you enter his home.
He hugs you and kisses you.
Finally, you're ready to tell him the truth.

You tell him you're pregnant and he bursts out
    laughing.
You look at him and tell him you're not lying.
He slaps you with the hands that brought
    butterflies to your stomach.
Now they bring tears to your eyes.
He says, "That baby isn't mine."
And kicks you out with nothing to say and
    nothing else on his mind.
Months pass, you tell your parents you're four
    months and you don't want to abort.
They kick you out because they can't afford to
    feed another mouth.
There's nothing you can do, but find
    somewhere else to go.
You should have thought twice about what you
    were going to do because now there's a life
    that depends on you.

I'll Tell You What I See (Critical Life Poem)

understood this student in a better way, and it was inspiring to see her share emotions and thoughts about her condition in a reflective way. In spring 2010, one student, Jesus, surprised everyone with his presentation of his Critical Life Poem. Jesus has been an underperforming student the entire year, not because of lack of skills, but because he missed so many days of school. He was not engaged in school life at all, and as much as teachers tried, they were unable to find a remedy for his truancy. Days prior to the presentations, he was absent from class, yet he showed up on the last day of the poetry readings. For his performance, he played music he had downloaded from his cell phone as a background beat to his Critical Life Poem. The students were thrilled and so amazed at his performance; he literally received a standing ovation! The class learned after that he wrote lyrics on his own.

This unit and the resulting student work are examples of powerful learning/critical literacy/critical media production for several reasons. First, the use of media sources allows students to make connections between music and traditional poetry. Music artists are not always viewed as poets, and rarely is their work integrated into the classroom

The Life I Lead (Critical Life Poem)

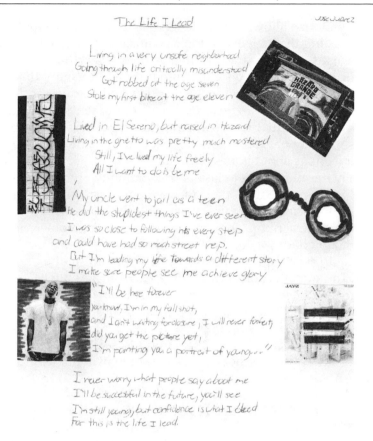

The Life I Lead   Jose Juarez

Living in a very unsafe neighborhood
Going through life critically misunderstood
Got robbed at the age seven
Stole my first bike at the age eleven

Lived in El Sereno, but raised in Hazard
Living in the ghetto was pretty much mastered
Still, I've lived my life freely
All I want to do is be me

My uncle went to jail as a teen
He did the stupidest things I've ever seen
I was so close to following his every step
and could have had so much street rep.
But I'm leading my life towards a different story
I make sure people see me achieve glory

"I'll be here forever
you know, I'm in my full shot,
and I ain't waiting for closure, I will never forfeit,
did you get the picture yet,
I'm painting you a portrait of young..."

I never worry what people say about me
I'll be successful in the future, you'll see
I'm still young, but confidence is what I bleed
For this is the life I lead.

for students to study and learn concepts. Music is a universal language, and using it as a tool for teaching poetry has been very successful. The students understand that music artists and traditional poets share the same sentiments about issues of love, life, and society's conditions. They can see how Langston Hughes and Gwendolyn Brooks share commonalities with Tupac or Common. More importantly, the students understand how these artists draw upon social issues in their writing and expression. Many of these works discuss critical issues such as racism, education, poverty, corruption, drugs, and violence. The students relate in many ways to the songs and poetry, but in this unit, they have to think about why these issues continue to confront certain communities, groups, and individuals. This leads to deeper conversations about their role as students and how to create change, which is a key part of the Agents of Change SLC.

This unit also allows for students to be both creative and critical when designing the imagery of their poems. When students decorate their poems, they also draw from the Internet, artifacts, and non-Internet sources. There is a lot of symbolism and imagery that comes through in their student work. Just as they did during the *Bless Me Ultima* unit, students know exactly how to represent the meaning of their poem with actual pictures and artifacts, or just media images. Students who are natural artists can use their artistic talent to represent their feelings about issues and solutions.

Finally, this unit builds a classroom community. Students share very personal poems with each other, and for some, just speaking in public is difficult. Especially for males, their ability to share with their classmates is quite an accomplishment, and it is a special moment for them to present a piece of work that is critical and reflective. Some students even bring in poetry they have written at home to share on presentation day. The students don't always view each other as intellectuals, but this poetry experience draws the class toward that perception. Bringing this experience to students is an opportunity for them to relate to one another and to produce student work that is critical and rigorous. Students appreciate each other and are proud to see their peers, some of whom are struggling in school, create and present about their life.

UNIT: PERSUASION AND CRITICAL MEDIA

The second standards-based unit in the year is persuasion, and students are required to take a district assessment, usually in the second month of school. For this unit, students must learn specific persuasive terms and language and write and deliver a persuasive speech. In this unit, Ms. Garcia selects controversial topics for students to discuss and determine solutions. The units are tied to issues that are associated with the Agents of Change SLC, so topics that affect youth, their families, and their communities are selected. For the past several years, students have covered the following controversial topics: gang violence, California Propositions 6 and 9, presidential elections, Los Angeles tagging injunction laws, and trying juveniles as adults in the court system.

The district and the English department guidelines require students to take the district assessment as well as to write and deliver a persuasive speech. Although the persuasive unit has evolved over the past 4 years, students have always accomplished the following final products: essay and presentation. The students' essays always include references and citations of text; students have to analyze quotes that fit their papers and explain and draw connections to their point of view. The writing process for the persuasion unit mirrors the process described in the oral history unit. Drafts are written and revised at least three times; modeling is continued with sample essays, topic sentences, and other key parts of the essay. Ms. Garcia also writes her own paper, which is used along with other student samples for students to refer to as they write.

One autumn a few years ago, students wrote individual essays on topics related to the book entitled *Always Running* by Luis J. Rodriguez. This book is about Rodriguez's life growing up with the influence of gangs, drugs, and poverty and how he overcame obstacles and challenges to become a successful writer and a better person. Students covered issues related to gangs and had to write a persuasive speech on whether or not gang violence would end.

Student Example

Have you ever thought about what our community would be like without gangs? Most people don't think it's possible because they say there are too many gangs. I think we can change our community if a lot more people have hope and actually believe we can make a difference. I would definitely like to feel safe and proud to be part of my community. Wouldn't you? I believe gang violence and activity will one day end because there are people who are willing to make a change and finally take action.... Somebody also willing to make a change is Pastor Cummings. He is truly someone to look up to and be more like. In the article "Former Gang Member Starts Ministry, Guards Against Violence Outside LA School" it states, "Students fighting because someone throws up a gang sign or the color that they wear. But every time something happens, he always there to stop it" (pg. 1). Pastor Cummings' actions make a difference in the students' lives. He helps the community improve its conditions by having less violence amongst students

—Jessica

The next year, students again wrote a persuasive essay, but this time it became an individual letter to the person most responsible for the issue they chose to write about. The district curriculum called for a letter to the school board, but Ms. Garcia gave the students the option to write a letter on a topic of their choice. The students decided on a list of issues such as immigration, gang violence, animal cruelty, tagging, budget cuts, college preparation, homelessness, and California Proposition 8. They had to present in front of school faculty and invited guests.

Student Sample

Dear U.S. Border Patrol,

My name is Jose and I am a student at Wilson HS in Los Angeles. I'm writing about how we deal with immigration because I see immigrants working in LA all day long, just to keep the city clean. Also my uncle was deported and I want to help him return. I want to support immigrants coming to the US because they have positive effects on America and deserve citizenship in this country.

Immigrants come to the US to work hard, cleaning for others doing many difficult jobs. I don't know of many people who want to get dirty out in the streets. For example, in the report called "Immigration Myths and Facts" by the American Civil Liberties Union states, "California, for example saw an increase in wages of natives by about four percent from 1990 to 2004 a period of large influx of immigrants to the state due to the complimentary skills of immigrants workers and an increase in the demand for tasks performed by native workers". This quote shows that because of many immigrants coming to the US during this year's, the people born here in the US started to earn more money. Immigrants are good to all people born here in the US if immigrants didn't come, American citizens would have not been earning more money. . .

As a student at Wilson I know that immigrants are a positive effect on the US. They seek citizenship and dream of a strong. Immigrants are hard workers. They come to the US to help us, not destroy our country. Our country should be helping the immigrants, not separating them from their families. We must stop building fences and wires. Let's not allow immigrants to die and suffer. Instead, let us make the right decisions by letting immigrants live strong and happy lives.

That year, the high school was also being consulted by an outside education organization to develop intervention strategies and courses targeting literacy. The consultant's curriculum aligned with the district's requirements for a persuasive letter. However, the curriculum also asked teachers to organize student debates on topics such as drug testing in schools and exit exams. To integrate a critical media component into this persuasion debate requirement, each group also created a PowerPoint with images representing the issue and students' position. Students could also use their own pictures if they wanted to; slides were kept to a minimum of two to three. The slides served as background for the debates and showed the key arguments being made by both sides. In addition, school administrators and UCLA graduate students attended to "judge" each debate.

The use of PowerPoint and visual images produced by students groups encouraged Ms. Garcia to develop a stronger media component within the persuasion unit. Students quite easily navigated the Internet to find critical and intense images that would relate to their topics. For issues such as abortion, the images were vivid and served as a reminder of just how controversial this topic is to society. It was clear that students could be pushed to further examine not just Internet media, but print media as well.

In 2009, Ms. Garcia introduced the Critical Youth Media Literacy unit during the general persuasion unit. This unit was designed for students to further engage in praxis (reflection and action) about topics/issues that directly affect youth, continue to discuss persuasive methods via visual images, build literacies via media, and continue to develop ideas about persuasion and how youth can take action (the SLC theme). The media is a strong enterprise in our society; most often, people do not take the time to be more critical of the news, images, and comments being made about certain groups, particularly as it affects youth of color. Thus, the goals of this unit were for students to develop a critical "consumer" perspective on the media (mostly newspaper and magazine), become the critical "producer," and make connections between critical literacy media and content from an English standards-based curriculum.

In addition to learning key persuasive terms and concepts, the class began answering general questions about media. The following are the questions used:

1. What is media?
2. How does the media work?
3. What is the role of media in society?
4. How do we analyze media?

After the initial discussion about media, Ms. Garcia presented students with two different images—a *Seventeen* magazine cover with an actress and a video game advertisement that featured a young male of color holding a large weapon. Students were asked to critically analyze the images and respond to the following questions:

Audience: How is the audience/recipient constructed? Who is targeted? What assumptions are made about the target audience? How does the ad/image/artifact intend to make the recipient feel about him/herself? What is an audience member compelled to do/believe?

Details: What creative techniques are used to attract my attention?

Values/Ideas: What values or ideas (ideologies) are promoted? What does it mean to be normal (or cool)? What does it mean to have power? What does it mean to be desired? Who is marginalized or "Othered"?

Thesis: What is the overall message being sent and why?

Student Samples

These images make me think that Taylor Swift is really pretty. This image makes me feel sad because I'm not pretty like her, but happy because she is on the front cover.

—Denise

This image makes me feel weird and sad because I feel unpretty. This sends the message that you have to be white and skinny and blonde to be seen as beautiful. This alienates men and women who don't wear makeup or look like her. This is a strange ad and they should have used a different model.

—Anna

After a class discussion about the responses and making connections to students' own lives, Ms. Garcia asked students to each bring their own artifact (print media source) to analyze using the same process. Students brought in a range of artifacts, from sports to celebrity magazines and other newspaper images. Students had the opportunity to reflect on the media's influence by responding to the following questions:

- How is the media representing youth today?
- What messages is the media sending about issues?
- How can young people critically respond to the media about fair/appropriate youth representation?

The media just shows the bad things about youth and almost never the good things. They call us criminals and delinquents. I've also noticed it's like as if only Mexicans and African Americans were criminals. It isn't fair that just because we are from a different country they treat us and label us as "bad". While the criminal rate went down, the media shows and makes us feel that criminals are in our neighborhood. I think the media work that we are doing is giving us a lot of information and the ability to tell what the ad is selling or something. I think the essays are cool because they are improving our writing skills and giving us more knowledge.

—April

I think media affects everyone in America. They are influenced by it, sometimes it's good and other times it's bad. There are many different types of media, like TV, newspaper, and lyrics. Sometimes the media tries to persuade you in buying a product or taking some sort of action. For example, when looking for a new president, the media influence people to vote for Obama. So you could say that the media is partially responsible for making Obama our current president but other times the media can have a bad effect by influencing kids to do something inappropriate and getting them in trouble.

—Alexis

In the second year of the Critical Youth Media unit, students completed the same writing assignment, but in addition, instead of giving a speech, Ms. Garcia's 9th- and 10th-grade English classes created a 1-minute digital video Public Service Announcement (PSA) on the topic of Arizona's SB1070 bill, which allowed law enforcement to require papers proving citizenship of anyone they suspected of being an undocumented immigrant (they also studied the DREAM Act, but chose SB1070). These issues were closely aligned with the Agents of Change SLC and also recent and controversial. Students had been talking about these issues in class and were familiar with the basic ideas from the news. Their relevance to the Latino/a community was also considered by Ms. Garcia when thinking about issues the 9th-graders students could be introduced to in the persuasion unit. Students learned about each topic from videos and articles (primary and secondary sources) and chose one to focus on for their individual papers. For the PSA, the class voted on which topic to select for the video. The idea for the PSA came from a 2009 UCLA Youth Council of Research summer seminar; that summer the students who participated in the Youth Council, several of whom attended Wilson High, made PSAs about their research.

Ms. Garcia was the lead teacher in the summer seminar for the Wilson students that year and knew the impact that this kind of media product could have on youth and their audiences. The PSA took about 2 full class days of writing the script and planning roles and at least 15 recordings to get the message that students wanted to send.

The 9th-grade video featured a classroom setting. The students wanted to show the bill's impact on eliminating ethnic studies. They created a script with a teacher conducting a lesson with students using a textbook. As the class read, one student questioned why other ethnic groups were not represented in the book. The professor attributed this silence to Arizona's SB1070. The students continue to dialogue about the importance of ethnic studies and end with a call to action.

The 10th-grade video focused on past and future scenes involving college students taking a trip to the convenience store. The students wanted to show how Arizona's bill was reminiscent of Nazi Germany, when Jewish people were forced to identify themselves to the Nazis. In the scene from the past, several college students go and buy some soft drinks; on their way out, they are the recipients of harassment by the security guards, who question how Latinos got into college. In the future, all the students are wearing "armbands" that identify them as "legal" residents of Arizona. They repeat the same action in the convenience store, but this time on their way out, they must show their armbands to the security officers. One student without an armband is taken into custody and sent to "Auschwitz." The students close with a reminder of how detrimental this bill is to the future of America and those who come here for opportunities in life.

The persuasion unit lends itself to a powerful critical media unit for several reasons. First, this genre gives students the opportunity to study controversial topics, including issues they have experienced or understand in a personal way. Studying a personally relevant issue has more meaning and engages students more fully. Secondly, the persuasion unit also requires students to do research, finding evidence, such as facts and statistics, to back up their ideas and arguments. Not only does this evidence strengthen their arguments, but it shows them how to back up their arguments with real data. Too often, students are not shown how to find evidence or critique information. This unit allows them to continue to research and analyze information, but also craft their own ideas and thoughts about controversial issues.

Integrating a youth *media* component within the persuasion unit further develops students' understanding and use of critical media literacy for several reasons. Students gain access to tools that help them better critique, question, and be aware of how media portray social issues. After completing the unit, students say that they look at their world more carefully or notice small details like colors in an image, whereas in the past, they wouldn't have taken the time to look at those details. Ms. Garcia can recall one student who said he noticed more billboards for alcohol in his neighborhood after the unit. In addition, students who hadn't been engaged in other classroom activities found a way to express their creativity and work with their classmates. On the day that Ms. Garcia's 9th-grade class finished the PSA, two of the students who hadn't been as engaged in prior work stayed after school to work on the video. They wanted to add a few effects at the end that they hadn't finished during class time. The students added another minute to the video, which included the students' perspective about their opinions on SB1070. On their own, they decided to film their commentary in front of a mural depicting activists such as Cesar Chavez and Rigoberta Menchu. The students were proud of their additions to the video and excited that their PSA would be shared with adults at the National Council of Teachers of English (NCTE) convention that November. The media component enhanced the work required of students in this unit: They learned the essential persuasion vocabulary, engaged in class discussions, wrote individual essays, and took extensive notes on each issue from both perspectives. With the use of technology, students had the opportunity to voice their opinions and share them with adults outside of school.

IMPACT

Incorporating critical media literacy strategies into my curriculum and teaching practice has resulted in many rewards and successes. I have established positive and engaging relationships with my students. I have learned to appreciate what students bring into the classroom and have tried to help them learn about and support their classmates. Each year, I developed more effective strategies for helping the most struggling students produce and participate in the work. The personalized activities helped students make connections to their peers and even my experiences. I also feel better equipped to work with students from all types of experiences. Some of my students come from positive educational experiences, while others have the opposite experiences for various reasons (i.e., discipline, moving, history of failure). Building student voices into each unit has given me the opportunity to help the most disengaged students.

—Veronica Garcia

Over the years, many of Ms. Garcia's students have come to her and reminisced about the time in her classroom or the projects and assignments they completed. Even the students who struggled and thought the work was too hard come back to say they miss her teaching. Their experience was one in which they actually wrote (and typed) papers and had deep and thoughtful discussions about issues they knew about and related to in their own lives. Some of them are also able to look at their old classroom binders, which hold their work from the year. They remind themselves of all the work they completed in the classroom and are still amazed at what they accomplished. Sometimes, students take their old work and use it for other class assignments or even as part of their senior portfolio, which is why Ms. Garcia keeps these binders. *Every* student ends the year with a binder containing his/her student work, whether it is notes, reflections, charts, creative activities, papers, or homework assignments. The students each have a tangible product to be proud of, no matter how much they might have struggled throughout the year.

Ms. Garcia's work with students has also had a positive impact on school administrators, other teachers, and educators across the country. Ms. Garcia made an effort to invite adults to her students' presentations. Their presence at these events helped build perceptions of the students as intellectuals. Too often, adults are not able to witness student production, dialogue, and presentation, but they quickly recognized the importance, relevance, and rigor of the work that students were engaged in. Seeing the potential for student work also debunked deficit thinking about what students can accomplish in the classroom. In addition, other colleagues of Ms. Garcia have become more mindful of using media in their units and incorporated some media concepts with their students.

All students are entitled to have access to these critical media and literacy skills, which ultimately strengthen their ability to better understand and participate in the world around them. Scholars continue to discuss the idea of literacy as a civil right, arguing that providing youth with the opportunity to be literate and have critical literacy skills can break down the school-to-prison pipeline, particularly for poor youth of color who make up the majority of this system (Winn & Behizadeh, 2011). Curriculum, teaching practices, and efforts by teachers that embrace critical thought and action can support these youth in developing the skills necessary to survive in an educational setting and social context that labels them as a population that continually fails and is unsuccessful.

RECOMMENDATIONS

There are several strategies that educators and teachers, in particular, can use to engage their students in a curriculum that is critical, powerful, and, most of all, meaningful. The following recommendations for teachers of English Language Arts can also be useful for teachers in other content areas:

- *There are ways to integrate a media piece into every standards-based unit.* Introducing a song or picture or video to students to complement the written text is one way for students to access media. Students' lives are rich with the influence of media and popular culture; most likely, they will be familiar with these elements and can even help teachers find relevant examples. The media piece does not take away from the written requirements of assignments but can, in fact, help students develop and shape their ideas.
- *Give students time to process, write, and revise.* It is important that students be given sufficient time to practice and hone their writing skills. They need ample time to revise and perfect their drafts. Students should not be allowed to submit papers that would not be acceptable at the college level. Although the process can be frustrating and time-consuming, it is important for students to have multiple samples of quality writing. These drafts should be saved and turned in with the final draft so students see the progression of their work. Every draft is one step toward a strong final product that any administrator or teacher can view and see that excellent work is possible.
- *Allow students to have deep and thoughtful conversations about critical issues, but be prepared to handle students' real experiences and feelings.* The success of Ms. Garcia's units came from the opportunities that students were given to discuss their ideas, feelings, and opinions in a safe and respectful environment. If teachers are going to open up their classrooms to authentic dialogue among students, they must be ready and able to field difficult expressions and conversation. Teachers must be able to facilitate students' thinking and experiences into social action and efforts that can start first with academic production in the classroom.

- *Creating and revising units that are multimodal, relevant, and rigorous takes a significant amount of time and effort, but it can help the most struggling students achieve.* Planning with colleagues and researching information about social issues and credible media sources is crucial for building engaging units. Students will appreciate the use of technology and can also provide teachers with ideas for relevant sources. For teachers who are new and unfamiliar with integrating critical media sources, focusing on one unit and making it successful can help expand the work to other units.

- *Take the time to model and teach technology skills to students throughout the writing process.* Many students know how to access social media and navigate the web with their talented technology skills. However, knowledge of and experience with even basic computer skills must also be addressed. Over the years, many of Ms. Garcia's students were never expected to type their papers and were unfamiliar with the computer skills needed to produce what resembles a college level paper. Students need guidance about how to format a Word document, set margins, place titles and page numbers for the types of products they produce. They need to learn how to type and insert citations and label documents. Having typed papers helps students feel proud of their final product because it looks professional. As adults, teachers know that work that is typed and formatted correctly is attractive and commands attention. It is critical for teachers to set the expectation high early on for students' work and take time to teach the skills that will benefit them throughout high school and beyond.

- *The support of other teachers, administrators, and outside organizations is vital—public displays of students' work matters.* When adults are able to read and witness students presenting their own work, adults' perceptions and ideas about students' academic potential are challenged for the better. Many adults have visited Ms. Garcia's classroom over the years and seen her students present at universities and conferences, each time becoming more convinced and appreciative of their identities as intellectuals. Too often, the media work against youth and only promote negative images of them; the work that can be done in the classroom counteracts those inaccurate and destructive portrayals. Seeing students produce high-quality work shows the possibility of classroom learning and success.

- *Make student voice the core of what matters most in the planning of critical media units.* It can be easy for adults to get caught up in using a variety of media sources and other technology, but what is most important is for students to feel respected and engaged throughout their learning. It is also important that adults use their media sources and other curriculum choices in ways that encourage students to think critically, rather than feeling put down or dehumanized in the process of learning or examining the work. Unfortunately, there are many negative examples and images in society of students, particularly those from minority and low socioeconomic backgrounds, so it is important for teachers to use media sources for a more meaningful purpose—student achievement.
- *Making curriculum and learning critical, engaging, and culturally relevant for students is part of good pedagogy; every student wants to feel validated in the classroom, but also held to high standards.* Just because education is embedded in a standards-based accountability system does not mean that teachers have to let go of creativity and adopt curriculum that is void of social issues. Educators who are willing to put in the effort and time toward enhancing their classroom environment will only benefit in the end. Students need to feel that their experiences and backgrounds matter and are integral to the classroom learning.

5 | Critical Media Pedagogy in Mr. López's Classes

In my early years of teaching at Roosevelt High, I began to teach elective Ethnic Studies courses after the local community organization InnerCity Struggle and its school club, United Students, led a successful campaign demanding that the school provide students with Ethnic Studies courses. InnerCity Struggle (ICS) has been leading educational reforms and working with youth and families in Los Angeles's Eastside for more than 16 years. Its mission is to build social and educational justice by empowering young people and families through organizing skills. InnerCity Struggle is a strong Eastside advocate that has secured ethnic studies programs in schools, led a successful college prep courses campaign, pushed for construction of new schools, and continues its outreach to thousands of students through educational justice workshops and organizing meetings. My journey in teaching elective courses at Roosevelt High began with my Chicana/o Studies course, which began with the pre-conquest and colonial era and ended with the Chicano movement and its contributions to Chicano/Latino people today. I also touched on current issues that are affecting Latinos in communities throughout the United States. Before covering pre-conquest history, I introduced the theme of identity. I continued to revisit it throughout the course because I found that the theme engaged students. When addressing the theme of identity, I often used popular culture. For example, when addressing the different youth cultures in the Eastside, students listed the clothing styles, musical genres, and artists that influence young people. They outlined various types of youth cultures and identities and followed their influences, such as corrido *groups, hip hop artists, and rock bands. Students read articles and engaged in dialogue about their own identities and the social groups that they see themselves as belonging to. Learning the history of Chicana/os was tremendously empowering for students. However, I felt compelled to also create a course that addresses the lives of urban youth in greater detail. My goal is to guide students to make more sense of their humanity and their present world and to learn to become participants in the shaping of a more just world.*

—Jorge López

Mr. López believed that it was crucial for youth to acquire the critical media literacy skills to deconstruct mass media messages and narratives (Kellner, 1995). The course, titled Youth and Justice, was a continuance of where he left off with Chicano/a Studies courses. The course began with the civil rights movement, covering the history of the Chicano and black power movements. Students read primary documents like news articles about the student walkouts. Students also read *Down These Mean Streets* by Piri Thomas, a novel that recounts the experience of a young man of Puerto Rican descent growing up in New York City during the 1950s and 1960s. The style of the book is street poetic, and it reads as urban spoken word. Mr. López had students reflect on urban youth cultures of the past and make connections to the present state of urban youth, going back and forth from the 1960s/1970s to the present. Mr. López began to engage students in youth research, modeling methods used at UCLA's Institute for Democracy Education and Access (IDEA) Council of Youth Research. Students conducted participatory action research, studying primary news documents, school yearbooks, and interviews of youth activists from the Chicano movement of the late 1960s. Students interviewed walkout leaders such as Carlos Montes and Vicky Castro and wondered whether the forces that led to mass student strikes in the past might produce the same result today (Oakes & Rogers, 2006).

Mr. López's students collected their oral history interviews and gathered their research and data into PowerPoint slides that they presented at a New York University (NYU) conference to commemorate the 50th anniversary of the *Brown v. Board of Education* decision with professors from UCLA's IDEA program. Students presented their findings and compared the experience and struggle for educational equity of East LA youth from the 1960s with current student experience. When presenting their work, Mr. López noted that students spoke passionately due to the real sense that "they are being cheated out of a quality education" and the opportunity to authentically participate in a relevant dialogue of their experience (Oakes & Rogers, 2006).

At the center of the course were themes of student rights and justice and injustices that communities of color have experienced in urban environments since the civil rights era. He used documentaries and music lyrics that are critical of various institutions and found tremendous success in engaging students using music and lyrics analysis as a medium of communication. He was inspired with the usage of youth popular culture and, more specifically, music media (Morrell & Duncan-Andrade, 2002).

Following the success of his course on Youth and Justice, Mr. López began to design the curriculum for the following new semester course. Having succeeded in his use of media literacy with the previous course, he wanted to ensure that the new course integrated popular culture, music, counter-narratives, and other forms of text and media for students to use as tools to critically think, analyze, and understand their current and historical experience as urban, marginalized youth and people. The course sought to empower students by employing a critical pedagogy approach centered on the critique of structural, economic, and racial oppression (Duncan-Andrade & Morrell, 2008). The ethnic/cultural studies course, The Latino and Black Experience in Urban America (see online Appendix on the Teachers College Press website: www.tcpress.com), depended heavily on the use of hip hop music and a few other music genres to enable students to learn the history of oppression and resistance in urban America. Because hip hop music began as a musical art form of resistance and empowerment for black youth (Rose, 1994), Mr. López felt that its use should take center stage in the classroom. His course began with the history of oppression of black and Mexican American communities and their resistance. Students listened to *corridos*, popular narrative song ballads from Mexico, to learn about the human effect of U.S. imperialism, discrimination, and resistance during the 19th century in Texas and California. Students also listened to blues and jazz music to learn about the struggles of African American communities and musical art during the Harlem Renaissance. The course focused on the 1980s and the central role hip hop took as an action and reaction to President Ronald Reagan's era and policies. Students studied the effects of poverty and the crack cocaine drug epidemic. They were introduced to the elements of hip hop and its popularity, especially after funding for youth programs was slashed during Reagan's presidency. Mr. López's class spent time studying each of the elements of hip hop and its art expression forms through graffiti art, music, and historical documentaries and interviews of youth of the time. Students learned about hegemonic institutions' attacks and attempts to disempower communities of color since the civil rights movement. Students learned how community organizations, such as the Black Panther Party, lost many leaders through police repression, incarceration, and the consequences that followed, such as youth gangs, crime, violence, and drugs.

Mr. López decided to craft the next school year as a two-semester elective. Each semester had a specific focus, but both focused on urban youth. The semester one course, The Sociology of Urban Youth Education, focused on youth and education, using multiple media tools. His goal with this course was to arm students with sociological knowledge and understanding—along with the theory and research methods necessary to understand why schools are underfunded and why students from poor schools are pushed out of schools at alarming rates—and to dissect the many ills of urban schools. Hip hop music media played a powerful role in the course, particularly in discussions of the challenges that youth faced in schools and what educators need to understand about the communities they teach in. Mr. López had his students read sociological and educational theory, including scholars like Pierre Bourdieu, Antonio Gramsci, and Paulo Freire, to acquire a theoretical framework and language to make sense and express their understandings of society and education.

Semester two, Sociology of Urban Youth, focused on various themes and issues that affect youth. Its goal was developing critical media literacy, and it incorporated an end-of-semester critical media production project. Mr. López felt that popular culture and critical media studies were crucial and necessary in the classroom and in public education. He wanted to spend more time studying how hip hop evolved from a more politically and socially conscious hip hop to gangsta rap and the current commercialized hip hop that dominates mainstream media. The class also studied the role of commercialization and media marketing to youth.

Although Mr. López lacked the basic media technology required to teach a critical media literacy course, he chose to weave its elements into his Sociology of Youth courses because he found it crucial for youth to develop a critical media lens, an invaluable skill to have in our modern, media-based society. In creating the curriculum, he had to assess the types of media he had access to and what instructional strategies he could utilize to present the material. Although Mr. López's background is in social studies, he went beyond his discipline's focus on history, politics, and economics and merged multiple disciplines, such as visual sociology, literature, poetry, theory, music, and film studies. In developing the course, Mr. López continually asked himself, "How can I combine multiple disciplines to develop critical media literacy skills in students?" As empowering as having the tools and knowledge to understand the role of media in the lives of youth is, it is even more powerful for youth to become producers of media. Mr. López's goal was for students to not only develop a critical eye, but also to become active participants in youth resistance cultures through the production of critical media. Morrell (2008) points to the words of Gramsci (1971), who states that "every class has its organic intellectuals that are responsible for knowledge production and dissemination" (p. 159). In Mr. López's classes, youth learned research methods and engaged with the community through interviews in preparation for the media-based project, where students took the responsibility to produce and use their own knowledge and counter-narratives of life in Los Angeles. Student teams focused on popular youth themes ranging from graffiti culture, gangs, homelessness and poverty, and flyer parties, to the spoken word.

HIP HOP AND VIOLENCE:
LYRICS, THEORY, AND REFLECTION AS THERAPY UNIT

This course not only provided students with college-level academic skills, but also served as a time and space where youth could address real issues that affected their lives. In the beginning of the course, students gained a strong historical and theoretical foundation, which provided them with background knowledge and a language to engage in rich dialogue. When addressing issues and experiences that youth live in their communities, such as violence and death, students had the opportunity to reflect through journal writing and to engage in honest dialogue. Students read academic texts, analyzed social images in music videos, and listened to musical lyrics related to the topic of discussion. In the unit on Hip Hop and Violence, students reflected on critical questions, such as:

- "How does mainstream American society view the deaths of gang members?"
- "What role does the media play?"
- "How do communities and youth who experience death and violence heal?"

Students analyzed the perspective of the hip hop community by searching for messages and advice on dealing with death and hardships. The theme of death and violence is a recurring theme in hip hop music, because it reflects the reality of violence in U.S. urban communities. These tragedies are often overlooked by mainstream American media outlets, except in news reports about the dangers of rising urban violence. Reading a piece by educator Alleyne Johnson (1995) in the *Harvard Educational Review* reminded Mr. López of the importance of addressing loss, tragedy, and death in the classroom. The author points to a quote of Freire's: "Education as the practice of freedom—as opposed to education as the practice of domination—denies that man is abstract, isolated, independent, and unattached to the world; it also denies that the world exists as a reality apart from men" (Freire, 1989, p. 69). The article reminds educators of the importance of understanding and addressing the day-to-day realities that students bring with them to the classroom. One of Mr. López's students who used to sit in on one of his elective courses was shot and killed during the summer of 2009. Mr. López began this unit by asking students to raise their hands and share stories of street violence. As the majority of hands in the classroom went up, students began to share their stories. Youth in Boyle Heights had witnessed neighbors, friends, and family shot and killed. Mr. López believes that, far too often, there is nowhere for students to mourn and make sense of their realities. In the *Harvard Educational Review* article, Johnson (1995) states:

> Looking at death only through a lens of violence generates silence around the issue of this death as loss. Thus, the tragedy and overall impact of death felt by surviving African American adolescents is hidden by mainstream society's inability and unwillingness to deal with the issue of death or with the brutal way most Black adolescents encounter death. (p. 219)

It is crucial for educators to address community tragedies. Too often, schools fail to address the realities of youth, and communities are too under-resourced to offer youth support services. Public-school classrooms can serve as a space for community healing. Mr. López screened the video and read lyrics from the Tupac and Scarface song, "Smile," and then had students extract quotes that served as a springboard to discussion. Freire (1998) asserts, "Literacy leads to and participates in a series of triggering mechanisms that need to be activated for the indispensable transformation of a society whose unjust reality destroys the majority of people" (p. 174).

Reading lyrics in Mr. López's class became an emancipatory process, where young people are humanized when addressing the oppressive, unjust realities of their communities. Not addressing and healing from tragedies is not only unjust, but also destructive to youth and communities. During discussion, students spoke about how they have dealt with death and the loss of friends and family. Many students in these elective courses were bused in from south Los Angeles; this gave the opportunity for students from East Los Angeles to engage in dialogue with them on their similar and different community experiences. In many urban communities, students lose loved ones or witness violent crimes perpetrated against fellow community members and never receive therapy or other services to help them heal and deal with the psychological trauma inflicted. For many city kids, their healing comes through wearing remembrance shirts and carrying R.I.P. art pieces in their school binders, the display of which is banned and demonized in many schools as gang related. Songs such as "Smile" and poetry on loss are, many times, the only type of healing mechanism that youth have access to.

Mr. López believes that educators have the responsibility to understand the communities they serve and the experience that students live and bring with them to the classroom. Mr. López feels that teachers need to acknowledge the experiences of our students and incorporate it in their classroom curriculum. Thus, Mr. López asks for student input to address their experiences with the question, "What can teachers do in the classroom to deal with death that occurs in the community they teach in?" His students believe that tragedies must be addressed and spoken about and that students needed to be provided with support. Music media is an approach that can be used. Peter McLaren (2011) believes that music "helps to bridge the gap between our inner and outer worlds, as difficult and agonistic as those worlds might be" (p. 141).

In this unit, Mr. López's students examined how a similar underserved community dealt with death and violence by studying the documentary *Hip Hop and Violence* that tells the story of a young man in Bedford-Stuyvesant, Brooklyn, who found healing after the murder of his friend by using media and creating a hip hop video with youth in his neighborhood. Most educators are not trained to provide therapy, but they can create therapeutic spaces where students can share their stories. Media projects and classroom group discussion of real issues, such as violence and loss, can serve to build community while providing a space for students to share and support each other in their common struggles. Shirley Wade McLoughlin (2009) believes that education can address aspects essential to humanity through what she calls "critical testimony." McLaren (2011) explains that, "The idea behind these critical testimonies is to acknowledge the oppressive circumstances surrounding the lives of marginalized peoples . . . and to create a community that can support the struggle for social justice" (p. 142). Teachers can provide examples of how other young people have taken action to address community violence and inspire youth to create projects, which can serve as both an outlet and a healing mechanism while addressing the importance of peace and services to youth who confront loss of a community member. Mr. López believes that educators can become powerful agents of humanizing youth who have, through traditional schooling and mainstream media, been dehumanized and desensitized to oppressive community conditions. Human pedagogy is about creating lessons and units that address day-to-day realities and empowering youth to encourage their neighborhood to engage in acts of love, peace, and justice.

CRITICAL MEDIA LITERACY IN POPULAR CULTURE UNIT

Mr. López believes that social justice educators need to be grounded in critical pedagogy and critical theory and be confident that students have the intellect to make sense of critical and theoretical texts. Mr. López began by reading from Henry Giroux's *Channel Surfing* (1998) and extracting excerpts for students to read in class, following with a discussion on the effects of mass media on youth and the commodification of youth cultures. The reading pieces provided students with insight on how youth are projected by mass media, which in turn affect policy in institutions, such as the criminal justice system and the prison–industrial complex. Students read about the demonization and scapegoating of youth perpetuated by the mass media. The text that students read addresses the concern that mass media do not highlight the realities that affect youth and their future, such as "high unemployment, dire poverty, bad housing, poor-quality education and dwindling social services" (Giroux, 1998, p. 3). In this unit, through multiple texts, activities, and videos, students critically analyzed mass media and examined issues that affect their lives. Students also viewed different types of youth-produced videos to see the power of youth in challenging dominant, corporate-controlled mass media messages and ideologies. Youth-produced videos are engaging to students because the content is relevant and real, and they provide a counter-narrative to mainstream mass media.

Mr. López began by introducing students to five core concepts (Thoman & Jolls, 2003) to use to dissect corporate controlled mass media:

1. All media messages are "constructed."
2. Media messages are constructed using a creative language with its own rules.
3. Different people experience the same media messages differently.
4. Media have embedded values and points of view.
5. Most media are organized to gain profit and/or power.

Mr. López provided students with a handout (see online Appendix on the Teachers College Press website: www.tcpress.com) to use in the analysis of music videos and all forms of media. The handout helped students learn to be critical of constructed messages and techniques. He guided students in questioning who created the message, determining the target audience, identifying the point of view, questioning who is represented, determining whether it is hegemonic or counter-hegemonic, and identifying any knowledge omitted. Using visual sociology, students were instructed to be critical of images projected, camera angles, sounds, text, and other visual images. Students began the analysis with selected videos and then chose a video to analyze. They presented their analysis to class the following day. It is crucial for students to have the skills to assess media that they will be consuming all their lives. Mr. López agrees with Kellner and Kim (2010), who assert that "the hidden curriculum of mass media's popular pedagogy, such as advertising and political propaganda, means that education in the United States, as a life-time process, tends to be controlled by dominant economic and political institutions" (p. 615). Mr. López's unit and course took a critical approach not only to media, but also to the role multinational companies and the dominant conservative class plays in capitalist America. He infused the course with critical pedagogy, using examples of resistance throughout history and media to inspire students and give hope to social transformation for social justice. Through the process of video analysis, Mr. López wanted to expose students to youth-produced videos so they could begin to see examples of what they might create during their production process. Some of the videos he screened were created by high school students and addressed issues of gangs, immigration, and family. He also screened videos produced by the television network mun2, which address youth in city schools on issues of immigration and military enlistment. For example, *Bastards of the Party* (2006) is a professional documentary film that examines the demise of the Black Panther Party and the creation of the Bloods and Crips. The documentary provided students with a better understanding of the history of Los Angeles gangs, the consequences of police and FBI repression for communities of color, and the actions needed to create a more empowered and peaceful community.

To continue to demonstrate the power of the media, Mr. López provided students with a handout of multiple images and logos from various corporate brands. Students were quick to recognize the symbolic media images and logos and reflected on the power and influence corporate consumerism has over their imagination, life, and cultural meaning. To check for student understanding and prior knowledge on mass media literacy, Mr. López engaged students in an activity created by the Global Action Project, titled "Media Relay Race," an interactive lesson where students compete in teams to identify facts about mass media outlets. The Global Action Project has a website (http://global-action.org) filled with many resources for educators and organizers in the field of youth critical media. Following the activity, students read an article on who owns the media, filled with facts on Viacom and other powerful media conglomerates. For homework, students were instructed to watch television commercials and keep track of ads that they viewed in one evening of television watching. The assignment also included ads on the Internet. Students had to keep track of commercials and describe their purpose and message in writing and prepare to engage in discussion the following day. Continuing the critical analysis of media, Mr. López screened in class the selected top-ten videos from MTV and BET. Students tallied images of the top-ten videos on a chart. Some of the overrepresented images included money flashing, jewelry, fancy rims and cars, women acting promiscuously, guns, violence, and clothing brands. Students were asked to take notes on specific images, song lyrics, or hooks. Semiotic analyses of imagery were not to be left out in the critique and deconstruction of dominant media. The chart was used as a tool for critical discussion of mainstream hip hop videos and their influence on youth. Using critical language, students gave a written and oral analysis addressing why the music is hegemonic or counter-hegemonic, focusing on race, class, gender, and age.

Music media analysis is crucial in high school classrooms, because music plays a strong role in the construction of youth identities and influences them on a social and emotional level. Mainstream music in popular culture is disseminated by dominant media corporations, producing capitalist ideologies and a consumer culture and society. Students found that mainstream hip hop music that targets communities of color hails, celebrates, and reproduces violence, misogyny, sexism, and a desire for materialism. By talking back to mainstream media through critical discussions, critical engagement in media analysis, and the production of counter-hegemonic youth knowledge, this class built resistance to cultural and ideological domination. Music media opens opportunities to engage youth in dialogue and reflection on the ideological topics that are often found in the mass media's master-narrative, such as greed, hate, hyper-sexualization, and individualism. Educators must create curricula that will assist young people with the skills to resist ideological and cultural control by the dominant ruling class through schools, especially in the current political landscape where they are attempting to increase their influence over education. Kellner and Kim (2010) believe that "school is often no longer a live forum for liberating dialogue, but tends to be a warehouse for knowledge and skills as a matter of transmission in which 'teaching for testing' becomes the norm under the banner of *No Child Left Behind*" (p. 616). Mr. López has found significant space within elective courses and core courses to create liberating curriculum and dialogue. Environments vary from school to school and classroom to classroom. However, we must continue to resist and push for time and spaces of liberation through transformative curriculum. If educators are teaching in very confined spaces of autonomy, something as simple as screening critical films followed by reflection and dialogue can be transformative and eye-opening to youth and contribute to building critical skills. Two films that Mr. López used in his course were *Sexploitation* and *Hip-Hop: Beyond Beats & Rhymes.*

The latter is an excellent film produced by PBS that critically analyzes manhood, misogyny, violence, homophobia, and commercialization of hip hop and youth. PBS created a companion website to the film for educators with resources such as discussion guides and other media materials and links. Mr. López's students reflected on the "discussion prompts," first through a written response and then through an oral discussion. In response to one of these questions—whether music artists should create socially responsible work—a student said, "I think artists should create socially responsible work and they should be more considerate of the next generations to come." Students also reflected on questions of gender, violence, and homophobia. One student responded, "I think hip hop is hostile toward homosexuality because artists try to act tough and they think that when they say words that are hurtful it makes them more of a man." The film and website are an excellent resource to help facilitate powerful student understanding of media representations and mainstream ideology of gender, sexuality, race, class, and power. Critical media education can provide students with the tools to filter mainstream, popular media and learn that media culture socializes and educates its consumers, who are often aware of its agenda. Critical media literacy provides students with the skills to evaluate media content, such as popular commercial hip hop videos and music.

Mr. López followed with a lesson on counter-hegemonic political hip hop, a genre that typically gets no attention from conglomerate mass media outlets. Students read, analyzed, and engaged in dialogue on the ideas and narratives found in lyrics, such as "Propaganda" from hip hop artist Dead Prez. The students' task was to annotate the lyrics, evaluate their meaning, and respond to statements made by Dead Prez in their lyrics. The class discussed the messages and ideological differences between the videos for MTV/BET top-ten songs and underground, politically charged hip hop/rap music. Students were asked to reflect on the power that music's messages have in shaping youth's ideological, cultural, and social understandings. Juxtaposing counter-hegemonic media with mainstream media was effective for Mr. López's students. Students learned to identify the differences in oppressive versus liberatory messaging and visual imagery and began to develop a critical lens to filter popular media. Mr. López's students developed an interest in and appreciation for underground hip hop music and counter-hegemonic documentaries and videos. Studying popular culture and hip hop in a school setting also showed students that elements of youth culture carry intellectual integrity and literary merit and facilitate their development of social critique (Morrell, 2004). The student–teacher relationship also strengthened as a result of teaching popular media. Students would often stay after class with their flash drives at hand, asking for songs and music from Mr. López's computer and having conversations about music and its messages.

The goal of this lesson is to develop visual media literacy through photography. This culturally relevant lesson builds students' critical understanding of their community through collective visual knowledge and analysis of the images that students select. Before Mr. López instructed students to document their community, he went over the "Visual Elements of Photography" to provide students with tools of analysis (see online Appendix on the Teachers College Press website: www.tcpress.com). In class, students looked at several projected images and applied the visual elements to build understanding of the visual meaning of these images. The lesson required students to document their community—more specifically, public places within the community that youth interact with. Most students used phone cameras for this purpose. Students captured several photos of public spaces in Boyle Heights. Then, using the photos, students prepared a presentation of their captured images, adding text and personal meaning to selected photos, and identifying the visual elements that were utilized. Students shared powerful community images with each other from their own lenses and perspectives. An excellent example was an image a student took at night of the Virgin of Guadalupe painted on a Boyle Heights wall. The student explained that the Virgin is painted on a wall that used to be a mental institution that is now closed and that "now is used as a mourning place to honor the deaths of the fallen young warriors." As students presented, they shared different community narratives, and many added a critical analysis of the places young people interact with. Units and lessons become more powerful and meaningful to students when they address their lives, culture, and stories. The purpose of the lesson was to expose students to critical visual literacy and engage students in critical visual production. This lesson can become even more powerful if the student photos are shared in community spaces such as art galleries, where students can share their photos in an exhibit event to community members, thus becoming a space for community dialogue between youth and adults on community issues and youth counter-narratives.

PARTICIPATION IS POWER: CRITICAL MEDIA PRODUCTION IN THE EASTSIDE UNIT

Students in Mr. López's class built their critical media literacy skills through a variety of lessons. In class, students learned about hegemonic forces in mainstream media and why it is crucial for youth to produce their own counter-hegemonic media to address the realities of existing oppression in urban poor communities of color. Students were grouped in video production teams to support each other in a collaborative video project. Students were instructed to think of themes and topics that reflect an existing issue, problem, or cultural expression that engage young people in Boyle Heights. Student groups were asked to discuss in their teams the importance behind selected topics and decide on one topic and create a video. They then listed who they would interview and identified locations to document needed support, challenges they might face, and team members' duties. Students shared their team's selected video focus with other members of the class for feedback. Throughout the course, students were given time to work with video production teams, researching topics online and developing interview questions. Mr. López provided students with guidance through lessons on developing interview questions, interviewing, and researching. He also connected teams with organizations and community members to interview. Mr. López determined the type of lessons and units to teach for the remainder of the course based on teams' selected topics. His focus on student-generated topics reinforced the relevance of students' projects and provided them with targeted support.

One of the video production team's focuses was on spoken-word poetry. Mr. López created a unit on spoken-word poetry, using poems by Saul Williams and Amiri Baraka as well as video clips from HBO's *Def Poetry*. Clips from the film *Slam* were screened to introduce students to the work of poet Saul Williams. Students used Williams's 2006 book *Dead Emcee Scrolls: The Lost Teachings of Hip-Hop*. Sitting in groups, each student got a copy of one of his poems to annotate. After they had finished their annotations, students were instructed to pass the poem to the right and respond to each other's annotations. Students could respond, question, and comment on sections of the poem or a student's interpretation. After this silent written activity, students were asked to discuss their annotations and responses in their small groups followed by a whole-class group discussion on the meaning of the poems. The goal of this activity was to build annotation skills and an understanding of the power of voice, interpretation, and analysis. The poetry of Saul Williams is rhythmic and interpretive and helps young people find both their own voice and the meaning and power of voice through a highly regarded, legit emcee in the hip hop, spoken-word, street culture.

Another powerful poem for students to read is "Somebody Blew Up America" by Amiri Baraka. Baraka, who has a long history in the arts of Harlem, is renowned as a poet, icon, writer, and revolutionary political activist. Mr. López had his students engage with the poem after viewing the film *Bastards of the Party*, following a class field trip to a Los Angeles County Museum to view an exhibit of the Emory Douglass collection of Black Panther Party Newspapers. Students pulled powerful and meaningful lines from Baraka's poem to discuss their interpretation and assess his style of poetry. This particular poem uses

"Who" to incite inquiry in the reader and, in particular, to question a
long list of injustices and evils. Here are a few lines from the poem:

> *Who created everything*
> *Who the smartest*
> *Who the greatest*
> *Who the richest*
> *Who say you ugly and they the goodlookingest*

This one poem can be stretched beyond a single lesson; it covers a
vast number of themes, topics, events, and current politics. It is a great
piece to begin class dialogue and to use as a beginning point as students find answers through inquiry-based assignments. "Somebody
Blew Up America" can be used in U.S. History, World History, and
any other social studies/humanities course. Three great video sources
Mr. López used in his Spoken-Word Poetry unit were *Freestyle: The Art
of Rhyme; Rhythm, Rhyme, and Life;* and *Russell Simmons Presents Def
Poetry.* After viewing examples of professional poets, students began
to model themselves after poets, hear reading styles, and most importantly, be inspired by the content of poetry. The course was built
upon Etienne Wenger's (1998) social theory of learning, where students learn best from finding meaning through experience, practice
through doing, community through belonging, and identity through
becoming. Mr. López wanted his students to create good spoken-word
poetry, and he knew that it could be achieved when students begin to
see and identify themselves as poets. His students began to gain confidence in spoken-word poetry through practice as a classroom community. Mr. López participated with students in the process of becoming
poets; one day in class, he played a hip hop instrumental beat and
began to "free-style flow" about life in Los Angeles. Students were surprised and impressed and became more excited and engaged to learn
how to "rhyme." Mr. López explained to students how he learned and
then encouraged the class to try a classroom "flow" by rhyming with
the last student's spoken word. It became a fun collective activity as
students took turns around the class, rhyming with each other while
storytelling. An activity like this one allows students to discover their
talents and passions for learning academic skills and growing as intellectuals, writers, readers, poets, or producers. Identity shapes how
students participate, and if they identify as poets and writers, their
writing and participation will go far beyond the classroom lesson.

Mr. López asked students to write their own poem on a topic
of their choice or on the topic they chose in their video production

teams, which included graffiti art, gangs, drugs and violence, poverty and homelessness, school conditions, and the poetry of Los Angeles. Most students chose to write about gangs and violence, expressing the struggles and pains of their Eastside and South LA neighborhoods. After the written component, students were expected to orally read or perform their poem to the class. It turned out to be an empowering, reflective, and therapeutic spoken-word session as youth embodied identities of poets applying their poet voice, rhythm, tone, and emotion. Here are snippets of student poems that express their harsh realities, hopelessness, and a desire to be the change.

> *Now open your eyes, this is what you ought to see*
> *Probably in ages, we'll recall how it used to be*
> *Until then, I can't smile truthfully*
> *Exhausted and bleeding, from all the deceiving*
> *People die from gunshots every evening*

—Jose Mercado

> *To beat up a brother*
> *To kill one another*
> *To strangle each other*
> *To never get along with one or the other*
> *"Violence" when will it ever end?*
> *Doesn't it make you wonder*
> *With the war*
> *Racism*
> *Gang violence*
> *Chaos all around the world*
> *Just make one think it has no end*

—Melvin Celis

> *Lay in my bed, close my eyes and then I start to dream*
> *Of a better world, of joy and peace, unlike what's seen*
> *People living in harmony, putting differences aside*
> *Realizing everyone's the same, everyone has a heart inside*
> *That's all that should matter, its what keeps us alive*
> *And because of this dream, it makes me wanna keep going and strive*
> *For a better world, and that's when it all become clear*
> *To make this dream come true, I must first rid of my fear*

—Jessica Pacas

The transformation of students into spoken-word poets is a humanizing experience. Human pedagogy is crucial in urban classrooms because classrooms can become spaces of human expression, creativity, and dialogue. Classrooms can be spaces of healing and humanization that can help youth make sense of their day-to-day reality and its connection to their inner self. Human pedagogy can bring hope to the hopeless and empowerment to the disempowered. A passion for poetry can be a bridge to knowledge from the world of poets and poetry. It is not only a form of self-expression and discovery, but also a confidence and skill builder in writing. Through spoken-word poetry, students can begin to explore new themes and issues of empowerment, community, struggle, oppression, and justice. Critical spoken-word literacy that engages youth can empower them to become involved in cultures of resistance and work toward social change. Duncan-Andrade and Morrell (2008) describe critical literacy and educative process as areas that "lead to actions, ideally collective in nature, guided by love and aimed at producing a more just society" (p. 27). Spoken-word poetry becomes much more powerful when students begin to interact with the poetry in multiple spaces and forms with the goal of lifting social consciousness. Spoken-word poetry can be found in many media spaces, including television, websites, music, and community spaces. There are many opportunities and spaces for young people to interact with the world of critical spoken word—opening up learning, contributing to the art through youth-produced poetic works, and redefining conventional poetry.

The spoken-word poetry video production team was interested in documenting poets from Boyle Heights and the greater Eastside. Mr. López was able to support the student group by connecting them to Los Poets del Norte, a spoken-word duo from Boyle Heights who share similar community experiences with students. Their mission is to empower youth and community members using both art and poetry that tell rhythmic stories of the Chicana/o reality in Los Angeles. Los Poets de Norte share their work in various community spaces such as schools, art galleries, community centers, coffee houses, parks, and cultural community events. The student group interviewed Los Poets del Norte and documented one of their performances in the local Ruben Salazar Park, which included performances by other local poets, artists, and musicians. The students also documented and interviewed the Chicana-conscious hip hop duo Guerrilla Queenz. Using the video footage, students developed a creative, musical, and poetic video that was shared with other youth from Roosevelt High.

Viewing spoken-word video clips from HBO's *Def Poetry* was engaging and purposeful in the classroom. However, screening spoken-word videos of community poets constructed by youth from Roosevelt High proved to be much more powerful and meaningful to youth from Boyle Heights. The goal of critical media pedagogy is to take students from analysis to production. Critical learning is transferred from the classroom to the community, where lessons of cultural struggle, gender, oppression, power, community, and voice are taught from community poets and musical artists.

A different video production team chose to document gangs and violence in the Boyle Heights community. Two of the students in the team had a family history with gangs. To reflect the focus of the video production team, Mr. López took students to Homeboy Industries, the nation's largest gang-intervention program. Homeboy Industries' mission is to provide job training, education, counseling, substance abuse assistance, and other services to at-risk and formerly gang-involved youth. The founder, Father Greg Boyle, provides youth with multiple support services to move them beyond gang life and create positive individuals and communities. Mr. López and the students got a tour of the site to learn about all the services that they provide for young people who have experienced gang life or live in communities that experience high levels of violence and poverty. Students interviewed a young man who used to be involved in gangs and was taking classes to build academic skills. Students documented his story and put together a video of Homeboy Industries and gangs in Boyle Heights. The video also included an interview of the mother of one of Mr. López's students, who used to be involved in gangs. This student took the strongest leadership in the team's video project because she had a very close connection to the issue and because her father had been incarcerated. Also, during the semester, this student was arrested and put into the juvenile system. She had to spend her weekends incarcerated in juvenile hall for the next four months. She became very invested in the project and created a video that shares stories of individuals who get "caught up" in gangs, violence, and incarceration. She chose not to tell her own story in the video but shared her mother's story instead. The video was an outlet and a powerful narrative learning experience for this student. She was determined to make a change and follow the advice of her mother to pursue education in order to avoid resorting to gangs. The video, ultimately uploaded on YouTube, became a tool to share the message and narrative to classroom peers in the hope that it will keep youth in the community informed of existing intervention and to reflect on the horrors that gang involvement can create.

Putting youth narrative videos on YouTube or similar sites creates solidarity with other young people and tells the story of gang life from the lens of a young person who has seen it. Mainstream media often demonize inner-city youth and the gang-life narrative. The sharing of youth-produced works in multiple spaces and on Internet sites such as YouTube can be democratizing in implementing critical media pedagogy for social transformation in new media technologies. Kellner and Kim (2010) assert that when the oppressed have the competence to address their authentic voices (such as students learning how to produce a video) and their experiences of social oppression, "marginalized people are likely to augment their counter-hegemonic struggle by consolidating solidarity with other social constituencies" (p. 617).

CRITICAL MEDIA PEDAGOGY IN SOCIAL STUDIES CORE COURSES

Teaching elective courses and therefore having fewer teaching constraints imposed by state standards has been tremendously helpful in informing teaching in Mr. López's core courses of U.S. and World History. Teaching elective courses has allowed him to explore his creativity in the design of units and lessons. When teachers are not teaching courses that involve state standards and testing, the possibility for creativity is greater. Although Mr. López is now currently teaching mostly core courses, he has found that there is still a lot of space for pedagogical creativity and critical media pedagogy, even with limitations and constraints imposed by state and federal standards and tests. He continues to infuse lessons with critical media literacy and engage students in and out of the classroom in multiple media spaces and in the community. Many teachers have never had an opportunity to teach an elective course, where the teacher has the autonomy to design the course. Rather, most teachers are handed scripted curricula or a set of standards that are continually monitored by administrators, to which teachers are held accountable through state and federal tests. Despite the current testing culture that dominates education nationally, teachers should not extinguish their creativity and desire to create curriculum and pedagogy that will engage and empower students. Students lose motivation and disengage from the classroom with a drilling, banking approach to teaching.

Curricula can still be relevant to youth culture, even with the many limitations that educators face, such as testing, standards, budget cuts, and the lack of technology and resources. Teacher layoffs and attacks on public education and teachers have created a depressing environment and low teacher morale. Now more than ever, when the mainstream media are attacking teachers and public education is when teachers need to utilize critical media pedagogy in the classroom.

VOICES OF CHANGE IN A WORLD HISTORY COURSE

Using media in the classroom engages students in disciplinary content while integrating 21st-century tools. Mr. López's World History course begins with a unit on Western political thought and democracy that addresses the 10th-grade history social science content standards. In this first unit, titled Voices of Change: Rage, Reflection, & Responsibility, students learn to compare important ideas of philosophers, government, and justice. Students studied the historical background and the ideas of philosophers such as John Locke and Mary Wollstonecraft and reflected on quotes from Che Guevara, Jean-Jacques Rousseau, Albert Einstein, and the hip hop group Dead Prez. Mr. López assigned each of his students a different historical philosopher as a character to study, write about, and bring to life in a classroom Socratic seminar. Students wore costumes and debated questions such as:

- How should we rule?
- What is the best form of government?

Once students had a good understanding of various forms of world governments and ideas of government by philosophers, students began to make connections to their own lives. Students reflected on questions such as:

- What type of government(s) generates more justice and equality for most people in society?
- How should society be organized to prevent social injustice?

Together with the English teacher, Mr. Dean, Mr. López created an interdisciplinary, end-of-unit, problem-posing project with the students they shared. Both teachers asked students to think about problems and issues in their community that needed to be addressed and to investigate solutions. The unit's essential question was, *"What needs to change to generate more justice and equity in Boyle Heights?"* In their English class, students used this essential question to learn to develop counter-arguments, analogies, and persuasive speech. Mr. López and Mr. Dean also collaborated with the math teacher, Ms. Perez, to help students learn how to interpret, analyze, and create graphs driven by their own data collection in their community. The goal was for students to learn how to understand information and use it to produce a persuasive presentation that elevated the social consciousness of the audience, utilizing multimedia forms. Students were required to research their community using interview questions on their selected issue/problem. Using qualitative data from the interviews, students wrote a persuasive report on their selected problem. In the writing piece, students included quotes from the community interviewees and government philosophers they studied in history, as well as quotes taken from texts they read in their English class.

To help students select a problem to study, they were taken through a narrative writing process in their history class, supported by tutors from the community non-profit literacy organization 826LA. Students were asked to write about hardship and struggle in their family history and community. The student narratives were used to find common themes of struggles faced in Boyle Heights. Mr. López guided students through "The Tree of Problems of Boyle Heights," an activity that has been used by organizers in Brazilian favelas. The objective is to teach community members to learn how "to see, to judge and to act" (Ferreira & Ferreira, 1997). Students were broken into groups to draw a poster-sized tree and then fill the top of the tree with problems they can identify in their community on the physical and emotional levels. Students listed the problems' immediate causes in the trunk of the tree, placing root causes connected to our government and economic system in the tree roots. When students can learn how to identify the causes of problems in their community, they can begin to draft what actions need to be taken to solve them. Some of the student-generated issues and problems included youth hopelessness, immigration, poverty, the Dream Act, depression, and gang violence. Students used their charts to identify community problems and find solutions to them. They also delineated the various roles that individuals, community members, and government structures play. Students used a planning actions chart to imagine a long-term vision for their Boyle Heights community.

Students were also required to put together a media-based PowerPoint presentation that included video from their interviews, digital photographic images of their community problem and solution, and graphs that reflected their data collection. Students developed eloquently written work that included the history of Boyle Heights, theoretical understandings of social structures, world governments, philosophies, and literature. The final, performance-based assessment required students to present their PowerPoint slides and speeches to an audience of students, parents, teachers, counselors, and their principal at a community evening. Mr. López prepared students by going over the elements of a persuasive presentation. Students dressed formally and presented their interactive PowerPoint slides, which included a description of their problem/issue, solutions, the philosophical government approach, and the projected effects of the change they proposed. The student-produced narratives were compiled in a book and published by 826LA, a non-profit writing and tutoring center, in a volume that was sold in local bookstores. The publication of the student narratives was a powerful action whereby the counter-narratives of Eastside youth were made available in major cities where existing 826 chapters are found throughout the country.

Students learned lasting skills that developed their civic engagement abilities. Public education should infuse its pedagogy with critical media literacy if we want to secure a future where young people will have the knowledge to lead and create justice in all areas of society. Students read news articles and watched youth-created YouTube videos. Viewing YouTube videos about student activism—such as the Tucson, Arizona, UNIDOS student group that took over a school board meeting to resist the dismantling of their Ethnic Studies program— engaged students. They were eager to document and capture their own footage and went outside the classroom and into the community, using handheld cameras and phones to interview students and other community members about their selected community problem. Course content was student-generated and based on the problems and issues that student teams chose, which included lessons on immigration, the Dream Act, and gangs, to name a few. Many students focused their presentations on the effects of anti-immigrant policies on undocumented youth. The national discourse on the Dream Act was taking place in Congress, and students followed closely both developments in Washington and the actions of youth nationally. Some of the students participated in phone banking to elected officials and joined the

Dreamers Club, a campus student group that advocates for undocumented students. Students also took a field trip to UCLA to attend an Ethnic Studies teach-in to learn firsthand from student activists and educators from Arizona.

At the culmination of the unit, students presented their work to family and community members. Students impressed their families and audience members with their interactive presentations, which they gave independently, one student at a time, behind a podium with a large projection of their PowerPoint slides on a white screen in the school's auditorium. Students cited philosophers, such as John Locke, and displayed the protest art of Ernesto Yerena as they argued the need to support and pass the Dream Act. One student, Horacio, stated, "It is a problem in society when students study so hard to have a future and will not be able to get a job. It's not fair!" Another student, Betty, presented on the issue of hopelessness, a problem that dominates the lives of many young people in Boyle Heights, arguing that youth need care to change the culture of hopelessness. Guillermo chose to focus on war and stated that he believes, "War is bad for our economy and for the world." His presentation documented the consequences of the costly wars that our government has waged and his dissatisfaction with learning that nearly a third of our federal budget goes to the military. Student presentations were recorded and screened in class the following day for students to assess and give feedback on the elements of effective presentations. This step is important in performance-based assessments because it helps students become better presenters by getting positive feedback from their peers and learning where they can improve for their next presentation. It also gets students used to seeing themselves on video and helps build their confidence in academics. Student voices should be included throughout the curriculum development and assessments. Project-based learning is a powerful approach for students to learn through hands-on work and an excellent and rigorous approach that can integrate critical media in any course.

GLOBALIZATION AND DEATH: A WORLD HISTORY UNIT

The traditional industrial revolution unit in World History classrooms focuses on the effects of industrialization on Western countries. Students study technological changes, population growth, and urban migration. Students study the functions of the industrial economy, labor, and natural resources. Most progressive teachers ensure that their history courses do not leave out the story of the oppressed, teaching students about the experiences of child laborers in mines and factories and the exploitation of all industrial workers. Critical pedagogy reminds us that curricula must be relevant to the lives of students and transformational in the direction of humanization (Freire, 1970). Teaching from the lens of the oppressed, the exploited, and the marginalized is relevant to urban youth living in poverty because their lives, families, and communities reflect that experience. Students come to us understanding that social injustice exists and enter our classes with their own pre-existing critiques of our social system. Relevancy to their everyday lives is the curricular hook that is going to engage students and encourage them to acquire a more sophisticated understanding of the academic language and disciplinary knowledge they need to become more powerful actors in their world. The historical study of the industrial revolution in high school core courses provides the opportunity for educators to make connections to globalization, one of the most relevant phenomena that are affecting youth around the world. Many educators are already connecting the historical exploitation during the industrial era with the exploitation of workers, women, and children in today's economic globalization in their classrooms. In this vein, Mr. López poses these questions:

- What are the working and living conditions of your family, and of global sweatshop workers today, and how are they the same or different than industrial-era women and child factory workers?
- How were conditions improved historically, and what is being done today to better working and living conditions for workers?

Critical media pedagogy can guide educators in creating a meaningful and engaging curriculum by enhancing teaching with 21st-century new media tools, furthering the relevancy of the curriculum for urban youth.

In this unit, Mr. López again collaborated with the English teacher, Mr. Dean, to develop an inquiry-based unit that explored the experiences of women of color who labored in global sweatshops and surveyed the Boyle Heights community's understanding of globalization and violence against women. Guided by a Freirian approach, they created a problem-posing unit that placed students face-to-face with the brutalities of global corporations and the consequences of their greed. Mr. López began his unit by having his students explore their identity by engaging in reflection and dialogue on the questions, "Why is my life valuable?" "What is my role and purpose in this society and world?" "How am I connected to people in the world?" He followed this exercise with activities that used poetry and art to facilitate the process of self-discovery and understanding the value of life. This unit's focus on identity reflects the belief that it engages students, builds community in an academic setting, and increases students' confidence in their ability to complete all the assignments in the unit of study.

When teaching the history of the industrial era outlined in the state content standards, Mr. López presented the content from the working-class perspective, making the curriculum more relevant to students who come from working-class families. In Mr. Dean's English class, students were studying the theme of the value of life, while reading the novel *The Daughters of Juarez*, which documents the accounts of *maquiladora* female workers in the industrial border city of Juarez in Chihuahua, Mexico. For more than 10 years, hundreds of young women who work for transnational corporations in the city of Juarez have been murdered and disappeared. Students were posed with the question of study, "What are the social, cultural, and economic factors that have created this situation where these killings continue, and continue to go unpunished?" Female workers in the city of Juarez are connected to all women who work for transnational corporations in multiple global industries. Every country that harbors these companies also experiences varying negative consequences to its workers and civic society.

In Mr. López's history course, students were grouped and assigned to research sweatshops in different countries, investigating the levels of oppression and the consequences of corporate greed. Students were instructed to research the sweatshops workers' wages, hours, and working conditions. They also had to find and list the names of the transnational companies that employed the workers and the environmental impacts and living conditions of the workers. Mr. López guided the class and provided context through multiple readings, some taken from the book *Rethinking Globalization* (Bigelow & Peterson, 2002) and documentaries on globalization such as *Global Village or Global Pillage* and *Maquilapolis*. Students put together a presentation to teach each other about sweatshops throughout the world, using an interactive media- or print-based presentation that included the global location of their country of study through maps, images of workers and people of their country, brands and products produced in companies, and wages and age of workers. Some students brought Nike and Disney products to class to demonstrate to and teach their classmates about how these products are made and the profits that companies are reaping at the expense of exploited women and children. Students discovered that many transnational corporations are allowed to operate with impunity, flouting social and environmental responsibility. They outlined human rights abuses, health hazards, mental and physical abuses, and the unjust levels of poverty wages that workers are paid. Some students shared stories of parents and families who work in similar conditions in Los Angeles, while others reflected on the many teenage laborers throughout the world who make the clothes that they wear.

Popular mass media construct companies like Nike as the "cool" sports brand to wear, making products by Nike very desirable to most youth. Researching and analyzing multinational corporations for this unit turned students into critical consumers. They then became critical producers of new knowledge and began to educate each other, deconstructing the image and message that popular mass media project to audiences and consumers about the products and brands of multiple companies. The purpose of advertising is to encode meaning into products to encourage consumption of both products and the cultural meaning of the product (Zollers, 2009). Consequently, students redefined the cultural meaning of the products that companies advertise, interrupting companies' encoded meaning and encouragement to consume. Students then re-coded corporations such as Nike as oppressive companies whose products should not be consumed.

Students performed their own research and created their own multimodal messages to present to their classmates. In the process, students developed their skills in research, oral communication, and language. Students felt connected to young people throughout the world through their clothing. In class, they began to compare clothing tags to see where their shirts were made, also imagining the faces and life stories of the young people who work in the factories that produced them. Students felt empathy, became more humanized, and recognized the injustice of people throughout the world being exploited by corporations that rob them of their freedom, deprive them of an education, and relegate them to a life of poverty.

Students read the poem "Two Young Women," found in *Rethinking Globalization* (Bigelow & Peterson, 2002), which compares the life of an American teenager to a teenager in a "third world" country who works in a Nike sweatshop. Next, students were instructed to write a poem in the same style, comparing their own lives to that of a garment/ sweatshop working teen. Students wrote powerful poems and read them passionately. Most students realized that they needed to be critical of the master narrative produced by mass media and its influence over the lives of young people. Some students were motivated to be more productive with their time when they compared their lives to those of young garment workers who work 12-hour shifts and cannot get an education. As a result of this unit, students will look at the consumption of products with a new lens, asking themselves where the product comes from, who put it together, and whether those workers received a fair wage. Educators need to teach units that will facilitate the process of making students globally literate and encourage them to become civically engaged in fighting for justice. Students who become conscious of global struggles, injustices, and their global family will be more likely to engage in civics and become more humanized.

At the end of the Globalization World History unit, students were ready to present the research they were doing as part of their English class. Mr. López and his students felt that students' second presentations should be at the local community space of the Primera Taza café. Students created PowerPoint slides that connected their learning from the book *Daughters of Juarez* to globalization and Boyle Heights. Some of the themes that students presented were empathy, the culture of greed, violence against women, and humanization. Students included data on sweatshops, facts about women in Juarez, and quotes taken from interviews of members of the Boyle Heights community. Through the use of social media sites, such as Facebook and Twitter, participants made their presentations a community event, where they presented a persuasive counter-narrative to mainstream mass media messages of women, corporations, and products. Families and community members attended, learning from the Boyle Heights youth, who wore formal attire and eloquently shared their learned knowledge. Crowds of youth arrived, some riding their bicycles while wearing ties, as their scheduled presentation time neared. Young people were the experts and the adults were the audience—which is powerful and transformational to the identities of youth and builds their confidence in academics and intellectualism.

6 Critical Media Pedagogy in Mr. Dueñas's Class

One of the first things I do in my classes is tell the students about my background and share a very personal story about violence that has been a very important defining moment in my life about two of my family members who were killed in a drive-by. (I gave them newspaper articles from when my brother and when my sister were shot and they completed a theory of gangs. We also watched a CNN documentary on gangs.) Hearing my story allows my students to open up. They see me totally differently, and the respect I gain from students allows me to maneuver differently. Part of pedagogy is being human. It is the pedagogy of humanity. Students see me as someone who is struggling, I see them struggling, and I am still struggling. My pedagogy has always been defined by my willingness to express explicitly to my students my own personal growth and personal stories to humanize the concept of oppression and open up the space for students to share their stories. When exploring their identities, students must constantly reflect on what experiences have made them who they are. When my students learn that I lost two of my siblings to gang violence and my sister was a victim of domestic abuse, I want them to reflect on their own story. Students know that systems of oppression exist, but sometimes they are not given academic examples of how these systems of oppression are enacted in the real world. It often is an abstract example that they cannot relate to on a personal level. The theme of violence has tragically and ironically bonded our experiences together and thus humanized our relationships to one another and led to student engagement with the course.

—Mr. Dueñas

ESTABLISHING MEXICAN AMERICAN STUDIES AT WILSON HIGH

Mr. Dueñas has been teaching Chicana/o Studies (Mexican American Studies) in the social studies department at Wilson High School for the past 7 years. This class is closely rooted to its origins. As we discussed in Chapter 3, Wilson High was one of several schools that was highly involved with student activism in the 1968 East Los Angeles "Chicano" blowouts that led to the establishment of Mexican American Studies curricula. Despite its prominent beginning and initial successes, when Mr. Dueñas arrived at Wilson, the Mexican American Studies program no longer existed. When a student named Joanne asked Mr. Dueñas how Mexican American history could be taught on campus, Mexican American Studies was re-established. During his second year as a teacher at Wilson High, Joanne had also talked to her English teacher, Ms. Quimiro. Ms. Quimiro and Mr. Dueñas got involved during an era of political activism that spread statewide throughout California in several Latino communities in the mid-1990s that initiated responses to the anti-immigrant law Proposition 187.

Ms. Quimiro had been a MEChA (Movimiento Estudiantil Chicano de Aztlán) club student at Wilson High School, and Mr. Dueñas was a member of another student club, La Raza Unida, in his high school. Both clubs had collaborated during this time when both teachers were student activists, organizing to defeat Proposition 187. Although the two had not been introduced to one another in collaborative meetings between both high schools, they met later and started organizing together when they both attended San Diego State University along with Mr. López. Mexican American Studies had been dormant for a few years at Wilson when Ms. Quimiro returned from San Diego State University to teach in her home community, but because of student interest and organizing, it soon became an established course on campus once again.

Joanne's enthusiasm affected both Ms. Quimiro and Mr. Dueñas. After speaking with Joanne, Ms. Quimiro asked her assistant principal about creating a Mexican American Studies class on campus and was told that in order to do so, there needed to be enough students interested in taking it and that these students had to be willing to be scheduled in this class for the following year. Joanne decided to petition students to see how many students were interested. Joanne organized a group of her friends, and in the summer, right before the fall semester of her senior year, they were able to secure hundreds of signatures in support of the class. These signatures enabled Mexican American Studies to be taught the following year. Ms. Quimiro taught the course for the first semester. The following semester, Mr. Dueñas taught her students Latin American Studies and she taught Mr. Dueñas's elective students Mexican American Studies. The following year, Ms. Quimiro's schedule did not permit her to teach Mexican American Studies, and Mr. Dueñas took over both classes.

When Wilson High started restructuring the school into Small Learning Communities (SLCs), Ms. Quimiro, Ms. Garcia, and Mr. Dueñas

helped formulate the SLC known as Agents of Change, which established four ethnic studies courses and a Women's Studies course as
core electives. For Mr. Dueñas, helping to build up the ethnic studies
courses at Wilson High School has been a very challenging task, but
one that has helped him grow as an educator. Mr. Dueñas has taught
African American Studies and Asian American Studies and is currently
teaching Mexican American Studies and Latin American Studies.

The importance of this brief history about the re-establishment of
Chicana/o studies and the establishment of Latin American Studies
at Wilson High is that these courses, like all ethnic studies courses,
are built out of struggle; sometimes, it is necessary to fight for them
by initiating and organizing a campaign (i.e., UCLA in 1993 and
Arizona more currently). The film *Precious Knowledge*, which follows
the elimination of ethnic studies programs in Arizona's schools with
the passage of HB 2281, documents the struggle students and teachers
from Tucson Unified School District's Mexican American Studies Program engage in to save their program from eradication. The content
in ethnic studies is very historical, but it is concerned with people of
color in the United States, whose stories are missing from traditional,
Eurocentric history courses. In the 1960s and 1970s, when ethnic studies was being established, students and professors of color felt that
the historical content in the American school system was Eurocentric
and what needed to be created was a narrative written from and about
people of color in the United States. Some argued that the ethnic studies programs should not just be a class within a department such as the
History Department in universities, but its own department. Mexican
American, African American (Africana) Studies, Asian American
Studies, and Native American Studies were created. Throughout their
history, ethnic studies classes have been targeted by governors, state
legislators, district superintendents, and local and national media,
who have labeled them as biased, ethnocentric, and anti-American.
Given this context, students have had to continually struggle to re-
tain access to these courses and programs. At the university level, for
example, there was a Chicano Studies hunger strike in 1993 at UCLA,
and on the high school level, there was the 2011 protest by students in
Arizona. What is the significance of this struggle? Mr. Dueñas always
tells his students that ethnic studies is the people's curriculum and
comes from struggle—and that they are lucky to be in the class. These
classes have a purpose that is different from "regular classes." Ethnic
studies classes show the history that is left out of the "traditional" history classes—the history that the standards don't leave any time for.

For example, students learn about the Chinese Exclusion Act in Asian American studies. One of Mr. Dueñas's Asian American students in Asian American Studies class did not know that Asian people suffered historically in the United States, and he didn't realize that Asian people have been in the United States for more than 150 years. This student told Mr. Dueñas that he never thought about his background, but that, after taking Asian American Studies, he was now beginning to develop his social-cultural identity. Developing identity is a significant outcome and accomplishment of ethnic studies courses.

THE IDENTITY UNIT

Whenever Mr. Dueñas begins with new students in his ethnic studies classes, he begins with the Identity Unit. He thinks that this unit is an essential beginning for ethnic studies classes because one of its key goals is to get students to reflect on their own identity, just as the founders of these courses did during their participation in various student movements. Identity is taught in this class through the lens of history, culture, economics, and politics. For example, one of the first activities Mr. Dueñas uses is the Labels Activity, which incorporates various labels that different ethnic groups use to identify themselves. These labels, which are placed around the room, include the following: Latino, Hispanic, Mexican, Mexican American, Chicano, Indigenous, American, Central American, Salvadorian, Guatemalteco, Asian, African, African American, and Human. Students are told to move to the label they most identify with and be prepared to explain why they chose to go to that label. They are allowed to move to another label during the discussion, but if they choose to, they have to explain why they have moved. This activity challenges the students to begin reflecting on their cultural identities; for many of Mr. Dueñas's students, this is the first time they have had to do so consciously. During this activity, students relate their personal relationship to their label, including their families' histories and whatever relationship they may have culturally, socially, and politically to their families' home country or their own home county. This activity allows them to reflect upon their own identities as well as their classmates' identities. It also challenges some of their own biases. After students reflect on this process, they have to read an article entitled "Are Chicanos the Same as Mexicans?" by Victor Mendoza-Grado and Richard J. Salvador (2003), which explains the origins of certain labels and beliefs some people have about them. Students match their responses to labels based on Mendoza-Grado and Salvador's definitions, which provide students with the cultural and historical context of identities.

In preparation for the final for this unit, students are asked to read, "I Am Joaquin," an epic poem on Chicano identity written by 1960s Chicano activist Rudolfo "Corky" Gonzalez. Since its creation, this poem has been disseminated through various forms of media, having been published as a book, featured in community newspapers, and re-made various times in film. This poem highlights the soul searching that was going on in the Mexican American community in the 1960s, making it a crucial piece of media to use for identity building in this class. As *The Chicano!* documentary narrator observes, "For Chicanos *I Am Joaquin* was a spiritual and cultural revelation. It was the history they never learned in school. It was a celebration of their Indian and Spanish ancestry, of their Mexican heroes, and American lives." Mr. Dueñas has modified how his students interact with this poem several times. He has had students answer questions about the poem and perform a "Say, Mean, Matter" strategy that leads to questioning and the search for deeper meanings of the poem. Although his strategy has changed from year to year, the objective has remained the same: critical analysis of the poem, leading to students connecting the author's struggle to their communities and their histories. The final project for students in this unit is to write an "I Am" poem that is reflective of Corky's.

Composing reflective poems is a struggle for some students for various reasons. Some have not acquired the critical faculties or ever found a space to discuss their struggles. Students have expressed to Mr. Dueñas that this assignment was the first time someone asked them about what was going on in their community. But as the students began to further deconstruct the poem and write their own version of what oppressed them, they made many links between what they are reading and what they have to create. Corky's poem highlights his view about the world around him. He begins, "I am Joaquin, lost in a world of confusion, caught up in the whirl of gringo society, confused by the rules, scorned by attitudes..." Students use critical literacy to understand the world around them and, in effect, produce their own interpretation of what their world is—which, many times, parallels Corky's vision but with their own personal touch.

This activity has resulted in some great student poems that challenge the injustices students face on a daily basis. It gives Mr. Dueñas good insight into how students feel others view them and their community and how they feel about their own culture. Common themes emerge from students' stories. A recurring theme that appears in student poems is violence and its effect on the youth and their communities. Even if students identify gangs as a problem, they don't know why and how things got to be this way in their communities. At this point in developing a critical consciousness, some students are, for the first time, being exposed to the concepts of oppression that are directly connected to their own personal histories and ancestors, so it helps students to start with themselves and then connect with their history.

INDIGENOUS CULTURES OF LATIN AMERICA

The second unit Mr. Dueñas usually teaches in his Latin American Studies courses focuses on the Indigenous Cultures of Latin America. The main purpose of this unit is to develop students' identities and their relation to indigenous people of the Americas. Even though not all of his students come from Latin American backgrounds, this unit's purpose is to connect Latin America with its indigenous roots and to deconstruct the stereotypes often used to identify indigenous people throughout the Americas. Many of Mr. Dueñas's students identify native people with the savage and warrior-like, overemphasized stereotypes of what it means to be part of native culture. Mr. Dueñas feels that his Latino students (especially males) either glorify the tough *machista* image of native groups like Aztec warriors, and relate this image to the need to be tough in the community; or do not see themselves as descendants of natives or as related in any way to their native culture. Learning about indigenous people is a foreign subject to most of Mr. Dueñas's Latino students. He wants them to consciously learn about their ancestors' knowledge and relate it to their cultures now. This has been one of the major goals for his Latin American Studies class, culminating in a major class project that will be discussed further later in this chapter.

Mr. Dueñas has found that there is a real struggle in finding academic resources for this unit. Students in the state of California are only required to learn about native people from Latin America in the 7th grade, which is only 1 of 11 standards required of students that year. Six of these are heavily based on the history of Europe (www.cde.ca.gov/be/st/ss/documents/histsocscistnd.pdf). As a result, thousands of years of history are jammed into one unit that may just have a few questions on the state standards test, so it is often skimmed or not taught at all. In contrast, Mr. Dueñas's unit focuses on indigenous culture throughout the course. Indigenous cultures' influence can be seen throughout Latin American history and is, for the most part, still a major aspect of the current cultures of Latin American people in both their home countries and in their history within the United States. Even though the culture is there, however, it is not always easy to identify by most in Latin America, let alone around the world. To have students connect with this culture, Mr. Dueñas uses many visual artifacts to bring to life a history that, many times, is seen as a distant or even extinct culture. This approach allows students to see culture that was banned for many years until it nearly disappeared.

In one of the first lessons in this unit, Mr. Dueñas has his students read and interpret anthropological information that describes the different time periods in Mesoamerica's history. Students read "Chronology: Mesoamerican Timeline," available on the Mesoamerica website of FAMSI (Foundation for the Advancement of Mesoamerican Studies), which is maintained by John Pohl, a prominent professor of Art History at UCLA and CSULA (California State University–Los Angeles) and an expert on Mesoamerican history. This reading outlines various time periods in Mesoamerica from pre-classic, classic, to post-classic. Students must analyze it in small groups and become experts on one of its sections. Students are also asked to teach their classmates what they learned in small groups. This activity shows students that the indigenous people of Mesoamerica are a grounded people with a long history that is well established and developed enough that there is higher-level academic material written about them. This reading also provides the students with good context for Mesoamerican history and helps the students when they participate in a Mesoamerican gallery walk in which there are pictures posted around the classroom for students to interpret.

Teachers can use different strategies to facilitate the process of analyzing images in a gallery walk. Mr. Dueñas uses a graphic organizer he created for his Mesoamerican art gallery walk to guide students and help them analyze the images and make educated guesses about what the artifacts are, their use, and what native group made it, and to describe the images. Students also have to write in the time period in which the artifact in the image was created. The only tools students have to answer these questions are their prior knowledge; a timeline of Mesoamerican history they had already copied; and a map listing the Mesoamerican regions in Mexico and Central America, with the names of native groups that lived in that region at the time these artifacts were created. As students walk around, trying to figure out what these artifacts are, some are reconnecting and others are establishing their first meaningful connection with the real Mesoamerica, rather than the stereotypes that are often portrayed in traditional media. In contrast to this media, Mr. Dueñas uses pictures he took in Mexico City at the Museum of Anthropology that range from stone tablets that display the writing systems that documented the history and astronomy of Mesoamerican people to gold lip-plugs with extravagant details made for those who were leaders and speakers. Mr. Dueñas wants his students to be exposed to the many elements of indigenous peoples' culture, hoping to humanize them to the students. He provides his students with information about the artifacts after they have completed the gallery walk. Mr. Dueñas tells his students that they are archaeologists for a day and emphasizes that they have taken on this intellectual identity by studying and analyzing this art for information about some of their ancestors.

The gallery walk process helps students become literate in Mesoamerican art and history and exposes them to their ancestors' art and culture. Many of his students really connect with artifacts such as the lip-plug and earplug, which are also worn by students throughout campus. Even the small connections that these photographs make possible allow students to relate to these ancient societies, which are the cultures of some students' ancestors. To further his students' knowledge, Mr. Dueñas and his fellow educators have established a partnership with a historian from the local city museum who puts on workshops where students learn how to read some of the writings, referred to as *codices*, from the Mesoamerican groups. Although the colorful drawings in the codices are often the focus of viewers' attention, students learn to interpret the codices as writing and to decipher their meaning. This unit provides meaningful and concrete access to knowledge that was essentially lost in Latin America—historical knowledge often considered irrelevant for educated citizens today. In a "traditional" history class, these codices might simply be pieces of information students would read about in a textbook and then encounter later as an answer on a state standards test. This is where critical media literacy is crucial in giving students the ability to interact with these artifacts, forge a connection with their ancestors, and appreciate these often-ignored cultural artifacts.

In the final for this unit, students become creators of their own media. This project has transformed into what Mr. Dueñas calls the "ABC Project, Moxtli Style." The ABC project (referred to by some as the A–Z project) requires students to list elements of something using all letters in the alphabet. Students complete their projects on index cards or any material that has to be linked together, reflecting the style in which the Mesoamerican people wrote their history into a *moxtli*, which means book in the Nahuatl dialect in the language of the Mexica (also referred to as Aztecs). Another element requires students to bring one of the alphabets to life in any form of media they choose, be it a skit, replica of an art piece, or dance. Students are required to present their ABC project in front of the class.

After students' presentations, students reflect on their projects, what they learned for the unit, and what they learned from the project in particular. While students are writing their reflections, Mr. Dueñas simulates destroying his students' projects in front of them. In his most recent experience with this staged destruction, he prepared a bag full of shredded paper and fake projects to destroy in place of their actual projects before class. As he shredded their supposed projects and simulated breaking the pottery that one of his students had created, the students started to notice what he was doing. Many started protesting, stating that they had worked a long time on their projects and that he couldn't destroy them. Some students asked if he was serious; as he continued, they started doubting that this was an act and became irate. A few students actually stood up, grabbed their projects, and attempted to hide them. After "destroying" their projects, he handed students their groups' grading rubrics with a "Fail" written large in red ink. When students protested once again, he asked them how they could have a good grade when their projects didn't exist. They were just shredded pieces of paper. This just added more fuel to the fire, which then led to two students resisting and shredding their grades and saying that their grades didn't exist either.

Mr. Dueñas then broke out of character and explained to his students that this had all been staged to introduce the next unit, Conquest, Colonialism, and Imperialism. This led to a class-wide reflective dialogue. Some students expressed that they knew that this was an act and knew what Mr. Dueñas was trying to demonstrate. Weeks prior, students had a visit from Amoxeh, an expert who shared with them the history of codices and helped the students to begin to interpret them. Within his presentation, Amoxeh highlighted the fact that the Spanish had destroyed most of the pre-colonial codices. He had also outlined the history of the *moxtlis* or codices to prepare students for making their own *moxtlis*. One student stated that she knew this was an act because Mr. Dueñas was trying destroy their projects as the Spanish had destroyed the Mesoamericans' books. Mr. Dueñas reemphasized that they had created their projects not just to earn a grade, but also to connect with the history of Mesoamerica and its reality. This connection between history and reality led to a discussion about the banning of certain books in Arizona that discussed issues of oppression and the history of people from Latin America. Students were able to make parallels between the history they were learning and the realities of their own time.

FROM CONQUEST TO COLONIZATION

In a unit titled Conquest, Colonization, and Imperialism, Mr. Dueñas outlines the history of colonization in the Americas and its social, cultural, economic, and political impact on indigenous peoples of the Americas, with an emphasis on Latin America, in particular, Meso-america. This unit sets the stage for a history of struggle that outlines the oppressed and oppressors in Latin America and how the dynamics of power have changed from pre-colonial times throughout colonial and current times. The cultural, historical, and political impact of colonialism on the indigenous peoples of Latin America from their first contact with Europeans to current times has been very destructive and oppressive. This unit relies heavily on primary and secondary sources, ranging from excerpts of diaries of the colonizers to paintings that were used as tools to systematically justify the unjust political and social system of *Castas* that categorized all people in Latin America in accordance with their racial lineage.

This unit transitions from the simulated destruction of student projects to a reading that explains the actual destruction of Meso-american books entitled, "Burning Books and Destroying Peoples" in *Rethinking Globalization: Teaching Justice in an Unjust World* (Bigelow & Peterson, 2002). After students complete the reading, they create a "found" poem using five quotes they choose from the reading to summarize its main points. With this assignment, students develop their critical media literacy by reading and creating their own interpretation of what they read. Following this activity, students are asked to perform a gallery walk of images of 17th-century illustrator Theodore De Bry's engravings along with images from children's books about Christopher Columbus and other popular artwork painted to honor Columbus. These graphic engravings of De Bry's were based on the writings of Bartolome de Las Casas, a famed Dominican friar, who witnessed the Spanish colonization of the West Indies during the 16th century. In this gallery walk, students participate in a "Say, Mean, Matter" activity in which they describe what they see (details about the image), make an interpretation of what they think the image is trying to express (what the author means), and identify why this image is significant (why the image matters). When students review these images with Mr. Dueñas, they begin to get a deeper understanding of how the Spanish conquest affected native populations in the Americas.

This contrast between the portrayal of Christopher Columbus and his journey to the Americas as a great exploration that has significant consequences and the images of the destruction of Taínos and other native people when they came into contact with Columbus and his men allows the students to see how media can convey different messages. They also begin to understand media's effect on people's perceptions of what is portrayed as historical fact and how history can encompass many perspectives. The transition between these images and the written text is very crucial. This "Say, Mean, Matter" activity is connected to an analysis of children's picture books about Columbus that give a very traditional narrative of the history of the conquest of the Americas, along with an analysis of the writings of de Las Casas, which paint a grimmer view of the conquest. Students answer a few questions suggested in the *Rethinking Columbus* text that help them analyze what perspective these readings represent and what message they are trying to convey. A third component of this activity consists of analyses of video clips taken from YouTube. Some of these clips are cartoons made about Columbus, and others are movie clips that explore some of the controversies about Columbus and his men's interaction with people of the Americas.

A major component of this unit is the analysis of the establishment of systems of oppression in Latin America—which is why it is crucial to have students start with Columbus, who represents the beginning of colonial oppression for the native people of Latin America, which then also led to the oppression of West Africans with the beginning of slavery. After students have acquired a foundation of knowledge concerning Columbus, they participate in a role-play that puts Columbus, his men, the Taíno natives, Spanish King Ferdinand and his wife Isabella, and the System of Empire on trial for the murder and mistreatment of the Taíno natives. This activity was created by Bob Peterson and is featured in *Rethinking Columbus* (Bigelow & Peterson, 1998). In this mock trial, students have to use the various forms of critical media they were exposed to and make an argument that they may or may not agree with. They are given the argument against their assigned character and are asked to come up with an opening statement about who they are and who they think is guilty. One by one, students say why they are not guilty, and the other groups get a chance to ask them questions. One student from every group becomes the jury. Once the trial is over, the jury deliberates, and they base their decision on the group that makes the strongest argument. This activity encourages students to examine colonialism from multiple perspectives. They analyze the culpability of the various players for the oppression of the Taíno people and, even more significantly, consider the role played by the colonial system, which was the basis for human greed that led to the dehumanization and near genocide of native peoples. The unit transitions from covering the conquest to learning about the colonial systems that allowed European colonizers to impose their dominance over native and African peoples in Latin America. One major component of this unit is the establishment of the *casta* system in Latin America, the first system of oppression in human history based on race, to set a context for students to understand the systematic approach Europeans used to establish and maintain their power over their imperial lands and subjects through the propagation of a dehumanizing mentality based on the belief that certain racial groups were superior to others.

Students participate in a simulation created by Mr. Quetzal, a teacher at Wilson High School, to experience what it might have been like to live under this type of system. It begins with a lecture to provide students with a context about the *casta* system, because the activity was originally created for students in a 10th-grade World History class in which students have more background knowledge. Students learned that the *casta* system of racial superiority was based on an elaborate ranking of the "racial mixing" of the various groups within the Americas—Europeans, Natives, and African peoples—that delineated more than 100 possible ethnic variations (Benson, 2003).

After the initial lecture, students were given two documents to use as tools. The first document explains the *encomienda* system, a feudal system from colonial Latin America where 3% of the population that is European/Spanish—called *hacendados*—control the labor of the remaining 97% of the population, which are primarily indigenous and African peasants and slaves. Students were asked to answer the following quick-write prompt created by Mr. Queztal:

> Spaniards were a very small percent of the total population. Why didn't the indigenous and the African slaves unite and start a revolution to overthrow the Spanish *hacendados* (owners of haciendas)?

Essentially, this leads to a transition into the second document, which explains how the Spaniards promoted the ideology of racism to maintain their power.

The second document, entitled "Spanish Racist Beliefs," outlines the hierarchical system of racial superiority for life in the colonial Spanish America. It explains that the Spanish are on top of this racial system of power in colonial America, with the Spanish-born or *Peninsular* being at the top and the American-born Spaniard or *Criollo* being second in line. Under the Spanish are the indigenous populations, who are seen more as children who need to be taught to be civilized and Christianized because they have a soul that can be saved. At the bottom are the African peoples, who are essentially seen as uncivilized and animal-like because they "have no soul to be saved." Students are asked to reflect and write on the following question while analyzing this document:

> How could Spain use this hierarchy to keep itself in power?

This question establishes the systematic connection among knowledge, power, and race and gets students to start thinking about the next series of activities that outline how the Spanish created a system of superiority and control based on phenotype and "racial lineage" to essentially maintain their subjugation of such a large population.

Students then participate in a gallery walk where they have to analyze the paintings created during the colonial era by painters paid by the Spanish crown to document and label the various racial mixtures in colonial Latin America. In graphic organizers, students list the *casta* name; describe the surroundings, clothing, and facial expressions depicted in each painting; determine whether they consider this group to be high, middle, or lower class based on the painting; and interpret what their job may be. Along with this graphic organizer, students are also given a list of various *castas* listing the racial mixtures and their perspective labels. For example, *mulatto* refers to the mixture between a Spaniard and a person of sub-Saharan African descent. When students are exposed to this system of categorization, many are shocked that people could be labeled in such a manner. The activity gives them an opportunity to reflect on the connections between racial categories and the establishment of systems of power and superiority. Some of these drawings show the more African and indigenous populations in poor, working-class professions; one in particular portrays a husband who is a mixture of African and indigenous cultures attempting to stab his wife. When students have finished this gallery walk, they are asked to reflect and write on two questions:

- What makes a person high, middle, or low class?
- Is a system like this fair?

Students then read and annotate an excerpt from "The Construction and Depiction of Race in Colonial Mexico" (Olson, 2012). This reading allows students to navigate and connect visual media with text and adds a critical element because students are not just interpreting images, but also studying the power of images and their historical realities and social implications. These visual tools that we use to maintain and reinforce systems of oppression express the dominant narrative and allow the students to critically analyze the power of art. In this case, the *casta* paintings are not only an artistic expression, but also a blueprint for the systematic foundations of a racial hierarchy. In analyzing them, students gain a deeper understanding of art's importance on a systematic level and its social implications for a whole population of people.

The students are then divided into groups and told that they will become part of the *casta* system. In these groups, students create cards with the names and mixtures of 17 variations of Spanish subjects in colonial Latin America. These cards are organized by racial superiority, with those having the most European blood on top and those having the most African and indigenous blood on bottom. Most students are uncomfortable about ordering people by these categories. "This is messed up," one student says. "Hey, I'm not racist," another student yells with nervous laughter. Usually, the talk shifts, and students can be heard saying, "OK, this one has more African blood, put him on the bottom. And this one, he is nearly full European, put him on top." Students devise a variety of equations to try to determine the percentages of blood each group is made up of, becoming part of this system of inequality. Mr. Dueñas reviews each of the groups' cards to determine if they are in the "right order." Students are eager to convince him that they have it "right," using their equations to highlight who has more power than the other. Does someone with only European and African blood have more power then someone with European, African, and indigenous blood? Students get caught up trying to resolve inconsistencies in the system to figure out who should have more power over the other, rather than just consistently questioning and rejecting the whole system to begin with.

They continue to conform when each student is given a caste and is forced to look for a job in accordance with their place in the order they created in the previous activity. One student is given the privilege of being a *Peninsular*, the Spaniard born in Spain who has the most political power. Three other students are assigned to the *Criollo* caste, a full-blooded Spaniard born in the Americas, ranked right under the *Peninsular*. These four students are the bosses, and they have to give the rest of the castes a job. The *Peninsular* hires for the highest paid position, which is a large merchant and is instructed to only hire people with the most Spanish blood. One of the *Criollos* hires the small merchants, another hires the farm managers, and the last two hire the *peones* or peons. Small merchants are also instructed to hire someone with a lot of Spanish blood, while the farm managers are encouraged to hire someone with a bit more African ancestry, reflecting the historical reality that sometimes an African person was given these positions to create more division among the natives and Africans. Whoever is left over is picked up as a peon. Prior to looking for a job, the workers are asked to fill out a graphic organizer to help them determine what type of job they would be most likely to qualify for. The bosses also have to fill out their own organizers with interview questions and also a section to determine who they are most likely to hire and the lowest caste they would likely hire from. Students really get into the job hunting and interviews. Some students jump for joy when they are being hired, while others complain when they are not hired for one of the better-paying jobs. The students who are assigned to peon jobs hang their head in shame. In essence, students are experiencing some of the ills of systematic racial oppression, job discrimination, and lack of good career opportunities for people of color. Students are asked to reflect on how they feel living in this type of system and to draw parallels between what happened in the past and what is happening today. Essentially, this activity and most other class activities prepare students for the final project, in which they develop narratives.

FINAL PROJECT: STUDENTS CREATING MEDIA IN LATIN AMERICAN STUDIES

One of purposes of ethnic studies is to create a curriculum that not only acknowledges people of color, but also includes stories about them that are often excluded from the formal narrative of U.S. history. The culminating project in Mr. Dueñas's Latin American Studies/ Mexican American Studies course requires students to research and create historical, social, and cultural narratives. This activity was modeled after and inspired by work that previous students conducted in the Leadership Development in Interethnic Relations (LDIR) class at Wilson High School and the UCLA/IDEA's Council of Youth Research. Both student-centered projects have used Youth Participatory Action Research (YPAR) where young people investigate important social issues and use the findings of their inquiry to advocate for social change (McIntyre, 2000). One of the hopes of this ethnic studies curriculum has been to make it follow the YPAR model, with a greater emphasis on race and culture. With the guidance and support of an outside organization, the Asian Pacific American Legal Center (APALC), and the financial support for professional development and technology from the UCLA Teacher-Initiated Inquiry Project (TIIP) grant, Mr. Dueñas's students have become not only learners of the knowledge that ethnic studies was intended to teach, but also co-creators/producers of these historical narratives. The Latin American Studies classes learned about the changing relationship between people and land. Students studied the impact that colonialism has had on all groups, indigenous people in particular, and the power relations between people and the land they live on. At the end of the year, students filmed, edited, and produced digital video documentaries about a food that they researched, how it is made now, how it was prepared pre-colonially, and its history and uses. In this project, students acquired the skills to use media tools to advocate for community health while tapping into their knowledge of indigenous cultures. One main focus of the student research and documentaries is the issue of healthy foodways.

This project came about through the teacher collaboration and student activism that had been brewing at Wilson High School. The MEChA students at Wilson and other student organizations enacted a Dia de Los Muertos Assembly for several years. One year, no assembly was organized. As a second assembly-less year loomed, Dinah, a student in the Asian American Studies class, approached Mr. Dueñas about making this assembly into a reality again after a class discussion about Dia de Los Muertos. Dinah and her sister Cynthia were able to organize several of their friends and other school organizations to make this assembly a reality. Another key element was Dinah's other sister, Xochitl, who helped organize her Mexica (Aztec) Danza group to participate in the assembly. She helped choreograph a danza routine to add to a play by Mr. Dueñas's brother Jose, entitled "El Dia de Los Muertos," that had been performed at the assembly for years. The students were able to organize a great assembly with the support of teachers. This assembly had plays, art, music, and traditional indigenous dances.

Throughout the years, various clubs, students, teachers, artists, and community organizations have participated. Drama has been a powerful element of these assemblies. Mr. Shock, one of Wilson's drama teachers, has had his students perform and direct the lighting for the assembly. Latina Unidas, a women's empowerment club on campus, usually performs plays that relate to women's issues, such as a skit about deaths related to domestic violence. Art teachers Mrs. Aguilar and Ms. Dabiri and History teacher and artist Mr. Ambrocio have been instrumental in providing a visualization of Dia de Los Muertos, making *papel picado* decorations and having their students make paintings related to the art and paper mache *calaveras* (skeletons). Several Spanish classes have created *altares* (altars). Students have integrated technology by creating Power-Point slides and videos. One example occurred when students Alejandra, Kim, and Kendi and their teacher, Mr. Johnson, created a video about the history of Dia de Los Muertos that contained interviews showing people's knowledge of the history or happenings of Dia de Los Muertos. MEChA also organized a similar assembly to honor César Chavez, which focuses on not only culture, but also activism and social justice.

Producing these assemblies has empowered the students who participated. It has given students a voice and a chance to learn about their culture, history, and current realities. This brings us back to the original reason the Dia de Los Muertos assembly was mentioned. The 2010 assembly led by Dinah, her friends, and student clubs, eventually led to the reestablishment of MEChA, which had gone into a 1-year hiatus. Students felt they needed to get involved more in community issues and learn more about their history. Increasingly, the students and their advisors became more concerned with access to fresh food and public health issues in general. Students met with their advisors several times at local coffee shops to solidify what their club's goals would be. With the help of their advisors, students decided that their club's goals would be to advance higher education, to connect to the community, and to promote health and cultural awareness. These meetings at the café not only served as a place for student enrichment, but also as a space of collaboration for MEChA sponsors Ms. Cueponcaxochitl, Mr. Malagon, and Mr. Dueñas. Ms. Cueponcaxochitl, an El Sereno community member and doctoral candidate at UCLA, had become involved with the process of re-establishing MEChA while doing her fieldwork at Wilson High School in the Computer Science course sponsored by UCLA. The sponsors' collaboration was instrumental in connecting the student activism to the classroom on a larger scale at Wilson High School. Together with Mr. Andrews, a Computer Science teacher, the MEChA sponsors applied for a TIIP grant at UCLA, which helped to create a collaboration and network of many teachers at Wilson High School.

Their proposal, entitled "Dietsense: Mobilizing Ancestral Memory, Modern Technology, and Student Inquiry/Engagement for Better Health in a High School and Community of El Sereno," resulted in a grant that funded Mr. Dueñas's efforts to take his Latin American Studies classes to the next level of creating their own media. Supported by APALC, Mr. Malagon's LDIR class conducted Youth Participatory Action Research in their community, and their findings determined that there was little access to healthy foods in their community.

This work also led to further collaboration among other teachers and students on campus to create a community/school garden: the People's Garden of Wilson High School. A meeting between Mr. Armenta (a social studies and LDIR teacher) and interested students and faculty members about his ideas of creating a garden modeled after his visit to a community garden in the 9th Ward in New Orleans evolved into the creation of the People's Garden. A group including teachers Mr. Armenta, Ms. Andrade, Mr. Malagon, Mr. Ambrocio, Mr. Johnson, Mr. Dueñas, and Ms. Cueponcaxochitl, APALC's Li'i and Lesly, and several students met for almost a year to formally introduce the People's Garden to the community. This multi-layered collaboration also led to the expansion of the presentation of student work by APALC to include not only LDIR's student research, but also Mr. Dueñas's Mexican American/Latin American Studies student research projects in its annual presentation of student work and in El Sereno's Community Health Fair. The presentation of student work has changed the face of Mexican American and Latin American Studies on campus from being one of mainly consumption of knowledge to having students participate in the creation of this knowledge.

Throughout the course, students build their analytical skills and are exposed to a history of culture and oppression. The videos that students create reflect what they have learned in class and what they chose to research. The main emphasis is to get students to create narratives that reflect what they learned in the class and their own personal realities. The Latin American Studies class is distinguished from the other classes in that these students pay special attention to culture and its historical ties to these foodways, with a major emphasis on how these foods have changed from pre- to post-colonial times. Students first studied these foods' origins and contents pre-colonization; they then interviewed community members, mainly parents who volunteer at the school, about these same foods' uses in current recipes and possible health impacts. Initially, the project's emphasis was food, but it branched out to include agriculture, *remedios* (remedies), art, and history using the "History of Coloniality" as one of its theoretical frameworks. In essence, students create a counter-narrative with stories that contest the Eurocentric model presented by traditional history. Students interviewed people in their communities and tapped into their funds of knowledge about their culture. Lesly from APALC, Ms. Cueponcaxochitl, Mr. Andrews, Mr. Armenta (a new member of their TIIP team), and Mr. Dueñas have all been instrumental to the organization of this major project.

7

Critical Media Pedagogy
in the Third Space

INTRODUCTION

Because so many of our most powerful interactions with youth happen inside of structured learning environments that are not formal classrooms, we wanted to offer rich examples of our media work with youth in what Kris Gutierrez calls the "Third Space" (Gutierrez, 2008). Why are these third spaces so important? Schools are full of opportunities to work with young people, and many hybrid spaces—be they clubs, or sports programs, or after-school programs—allow young people to make some of their most powerful connections to learning, literacy, school, and the larger social world. The formal curriculum of school marginalizes these spaces by their very name (i.e., extracurricular) when they are ripe with potential to provide the same kinds of opportunities for engagement, production, and learning as classrooms do. We also know that powerful after-school and summer programs allow youth to make tremendous academic gains. With that in mind, we chronicle several ways that the author team has taken advantage of these spaces to engage youth in media production. This chapter examines a MEChA club that employs critical drama as a social action strategy, an Art Club that uses murals as a form of community education, and a research club where youth use media to inform peers and administrators about important educational issues.

The final section of this chapter will show what is possible in extended day and summer spaces with respect to the development of digital literacies and civic engagement. We explore a 12-year, multi-school project, directed by Mr. Morrell—called the Council of Youth Research—that involves city youth in the project of collecting and disseminating research related to the conditions of city schools. Since 1999, these youth have conducted action research projects on life in schools and communities. The high-school-aged students have conducted interviews, distributed surveys, and visited schools, neighborhood centers, and policy arenas. They have created research reports, news articles, blogs, essays, PowerPoint presentations, and digital documentaries. They have presented their work at Los Angeles City Hall, the State Capitol, universities, and national research conferences throughout the United States. They have also presented their work virtually through blogs, Ning sites, Facebook, YouTube, and a university institute's website. They have been covered by local and national media such as CNN, the *Los Angeles Times*, KPCC, *La Opinion*, New America Media, and the *Los Angeles Daily News*, to name a few. Specifically, we will analyze the role of documentary filmmaking in the Youth Council's mission. How did the members of the youth council become digital filmmakers? What academic, new media, and civic literacies did they develop in this process? How did students involved in the Youth Council employ their digital documentaries in their action for social change?

CRITICAL DRAMA AND COMMUNITY ACTION AT WILSON

It was not until the advent of the Chicano Movement that the idea of Chicano Studies first began in California in the aftermath of the Los Angeles school blowouts of 1967–68. From these school protests came the demand for Chicano Studies courses and the rise in the interest in studying the Chicano experience. In 1968, the California State University, Los Angeles became the first post-secondary institution to establish a department of Mexican American Studies. Several other campuses followed suit the following year with an assortment of centers and programs. By the early 1970s, there were programs in several other states, particularly Texas.

The main stimulus for Chicano Studies came from a conference at the University of California, Santa Barbara, sponsored by the Chicano Coordinating Committee on Higher Education. Also from the conference came the idea of forming the student group Movimiento Estudiantil Chicano de Aztlan (MEChA) and the creation of Chicano Studies as an academic pursuit. The organization of both agendas was outlined in the "Plan de Santa Barbara," an educational blueprint that called for institutional reform within the "context of politics for change." (Maciel & Ortiz, 1996, p. 183)

Critical third spaces at Wilson have worked independently and also in conjunction with classroom instruction to create critical media for the school-wide community. Mr. Dueñas has been the sponsor of the school's MEChA club for most of his teaching career and has seen this club consistently create awareness of the cultural roots and history among students while also exposing them to political activism. Every year, the dynamics of students who join MEChA change, but in essence, its goals, purpose, and spirit stay the same; its goal is to create positive change for the school, its students, and its environment. As mentioned in Chapter 6, MEChA's activism on campus led to the development of a Mexican American Studies curriculum. MEChA itself is a creation of the student movement that organized and walked out of schools at Wilson, Lincoln, Roosevelt, and Garfield with demands that schools teach students about their culture. Out of this student activist spirit in East Los Angeles in 1968, Chicano Studies was created. This history, then, reemphasizes the need for critical third spaces to create change in and out of the classroom. The relationship between students' activism and Chicano Studies at Wilson is reciprocal. Two major events MEChA has organized for several years at Wilson are the Dia de Los Muertos assembly and the César E. Chavez assembly. Producing these assemblies has led to many collaborative movements on campus. Most recently, the creation of a community garden and a collaborative interdisciplinary project that is funded by UCLA's TIIP grant evolved into a strong, critical third space that merged academic content with an after-school club and an out-of-school community project. The MEChA club members at Wilson were a major part in both initiatives, which also had a reciprocal relationship. At Wilson's People's Garden Planting Festival, Mr. Dueñas and his students read the following speech, which gives a good outline on how this all came about:

> The journey began for this garden as individual thoughts and has flourished into collective action. It all started with the research of some students in a class here at Wilson called LDIR (Leadership Development in Interethnic Relations). They revealed that the surrounding communities have very little access to organic fruits and vegetables, specifically healthy foods. Another group of students had emerged to reestablish the MEChA club on campus. This group of students had set forth their goals for MEChA as connecting with the community, promoting culture and pursuing a higher education. As the LDIR class provided the data that revealed the truth about the crisis of our community and MEChA provided the activism to do something for and with our communities, these

two groups seemed destined to create something great. One of the LDIR teachers, Mr. Armenta, visited New Orleans and saw a community garden that he felt was something that we could do here at Wilson. A few teachers at Wilson received a grant from UCLA called the TIIP grant to promote healthy foods using culture and technology. All the pieces of the puzzle were falling into place. It is then that we decided we were going to create a community garden. For a year, we had several meetings going over and over the details of our garden with students, teachers, and community members. With the great support of APALC (Asian Pacific American Legal Center) and after months of preparation, votes, mission and vision creating, garden naming, etc., we finally were ready to create our garden. A month ago, we broke ground and started the real work. For the past weeks, teachers, APALC members, and students have worked countless hours to get to where we are now, this beautiful garden built with a lot of love. This is our grand opening and planting ceremony. This is not the beginning nor is it the end of our garden. We will continue working hard with everyone and we invite everyone to come join us and partake in our dream.

This collaboration among students, teachers, and community organizations not only created strong relationships with those involved, but also fostered a variety of collaborations between teachers and students and initiated a variety of new projects. Key to this collaboration is student activism and the production of critical media, which has empowered the students to inspire and educate others. At the core of all of the initiatives that Mr. Dueñas organized is the participation of students. It was students who asserted the need to learn about their histories and helped organize the reestablishment of Mexican American Studies. It was students who did the research that found the need in the community to have access to healthier food in their communities that eventually led to the establishment of the People's Garden at Wilson. It was the students who created the production of plays, skits, poems, and music to communicate their culture to the school community. The teachers were the facilitators of this process, and their will to help create and build upon these students' ideas was very important. When adults ignore what the youth want to create and see themselves as all-knowing, it slows and, at times, halts the growth of student learning. The actions of the students are noticed by the larger community. On one day in particular a school newspaper's heading reads, "Food for thought: Wilson students to fast to honor Cesar Chavez and bring awareness to issues."

In another article, the heading reads, "An event to remember: Assembly celebrates the legacy of Cesar Chavez." Teachers from several Small Learning Communities at Wilson, the MEChA club, and other students developed a series of events that included a mural painting, a day-long fast for justice, and an assembly commemorating César E. Chavez and his spirit of activism. These spaces were created in collaboration with students and teachers. What to some may be a simple play or mural painting is often one of the most powerful pieces of critical media. The restrictive time limits and curricular constraints imposed by the school can often be remedied by collaboration outside of the classroom.

For 3 years, Ms. Garcia served as a lead teacher for the Wilson team of the Council of Youth Research (CYR) in both the school year and summer programs. This lead teacher role was designed to support and guide students in their development of a critical educational research project. Each year in both settings, the group produced a multimedia PowerPoint presentation and short 1-minute documentary and/or Public Service Announcement that they would share with various audiences at public forums and local and national conferences for educators. The students would also share their media products via the project website and social media outlets such as Facebook, YouTube, and Ning. For several years, this student group was unlike any at Wilson High due to its participatory action research model and the critical nature of the work students undertook to learn education and social theories, ask questions about their school, interview school faculty and students, and have the opportunity to present their work both locally and across the nation. Over the years, seven students participated with Ms. Garcia at Wilson and represented Wilson High School in the city-wide summer program, with several staying in the group for 3 years.

During the school year, weekly after-school meetings were held on campus and on weekends at UCLA and the local coffee shop in El Sereno. Meetings were also attended by Ms. Mirra, the UCLA program coordinator. The ratio of two adults to five students was ideal given the intensity of the research project and the ambitious goals of the Youth Council. Often, students needed individual attention on either their research or their writing, and Ms. Mirra and Ms. Garcia were often able to divide and conquer. Additionally, two adults meant that students would be given even more personal support throughout their involvement in CYR because the program resembled a family, given the small number of students and their long-term involvement with the Youth Council.

The students first learned theories of education and sociology to understand how these ideas connected to their research and the conditions they studied in their schools. They had to learn ethnographic research terms in order to know how to carry out their projects. The students spent many hours interviewing students and family members in their neighborhoods and all over Los Angeles to develop their training as ethnographic researchers. These field experiences allowed them to capture hours of video footage and hundreds of pictures documenting significant moments with individuals in the community. The students had to learn how to edit and revise their footage and select pictures that were most telling of the stories they wanted to share. They also learned how to organize and understand data. The students collected hundreds of surveys (both as a school team and within the larger CYR, which consisted of six high school teams across the city) to analyze for trends, which required understanding computer programs such as Microsoft Excel and making charts and graphs for their PowerPoint slides. They had to learn how to craft statements that represented their data in a succinct and clear way for both students and adults to understand. Lastly, the students learned how to make presentations for both local and national audiences. They had to practice in front of one another and, at times, with other teachers at Wilson who were willing to attend a practice run. The following presentations were completed by the Wilson students: 2007–2008, Students as Architects; 2008–2009, Critical Researchers Investigating Solutions in Society (Crisis); and 2009–2010, One Step Forward, Two Steps Back: Stressful Times at Wilson High School. For each presentation, Ms. Garcia and Ms. Mirra helped guide the students in developing the final product each year. The students, however, had the larger role in determining their main findings and how to present them.

The Wilson CYR is an example of a powerful third space for critical media production that provides students with both academic and social benefits. *CYR engaged students in higher-order thinking and critical analysis of information, data, and many other texts.* Students learned how to think critically and analyze real, live footage and images, as well as qualitative and quantitative data gathered from both surveys and interviews. Many students commented that this group was harder than most of their classes. This experience for the students was new, challenging, and even uncomfortable at times because they had never done this type of work. There are few instances where young people get to examine and critique information about their own schools and communities with their teachers and other adults. Students had to learn theories and read texts that are not usually taught until graduate school. They became familiar with the names of such educational scholars as Paulo Freire and Daniel Solórzano and began to use them with ease and confidence. Unfortunately, not enough teachers challenge and push their students to work and think in this difficult but empowering manner. For some of our students to only experience this type of rigor in the program and not in their classes is symptomatic of the low expectations that the school system has for students—particularly students of color from low-income communities.

Students improved their media literacy skills, but also gained new ways of interacting with media for social justice and advocacy purposes (to support themselves and others). The student researchers accessed different social media sites and resources in their pursuit of data and information for their projects. Some of the websites they found were centered in their own communities. For the East LA students, for example, places such as Barrio Action or United Students at InnerCity Struggle in the community were unknown to them at the beginning of the seminar. As the students began their research projects and visited sites to conduct interviews with staff, they became aware of individuals and resources available to help them, their families, and schools. The websites became real spaces with real individuals, both adults and students, where advocacy for their communities was at the heart of their mission and vision. Over the years in the CYR seminar and school program, students frequented these places, both on the web and in person, and developed a stronger and more critical awareness of social media and advocacy.

Students changed their perceptions of themselves as intellectuals and gained confidence. Participating in CYR required students to work on editing their presentations constantly until the final product was polished and of high quality. This often required them to meet in the evenings at the café or at each other's homes to finish their work. While this task was frustrating for the students, it showed them just how hard they should be expected to work *every* day in school. Too often, students are given assignments and turn in one draft at most, leaving errors uncorrected. These students go through school having few papers or assignments that truly represent high-quality work. CYR provided the opportunity to push a small group of students to their highest potential. One day or week of research amounted to hours of editing and putting together their data. Much time was spent listening to interviews, coding for themes, and capturing quotes. They were forced to think hard about their data and ask themselves questions about the results. Ms. Garcia and the UCLA staff made sure that the students' work could be shown to any audience, demonstrating that youth of color can work at a high level when they are supported and held to a high standard. The final presentations represented the culmination of hours of stressful work— often coming down to the final hour, at times pushing students to revise and take their projects to another level after they felt their work was completed. The students in the group all had average academic backgrounds, and some had even failed certain classes. Yet their participation in CYR changed their beliefs about themselves, and with help from each other, Ms. Garcia, and the CYR support staff, they turned their grades around for the better. Over time, students felt confident in their knowledge and believed that their own ideas, experiences, and opinions were relevant and valid. They were "experts" on the data and saw themselves as stronger students than ever before. Creating that spark of interest requires time and energy of educators, but ultimately results in powerful learning and even life-changing experiences for students.

Students' opportunities to share their knowledge of education in issues in public spaces increased. The work of CYR in both the summer and school programs became of greater interest to local school and district administrators as students presented at City Hall, at the district offices, on university campuses, and in their own schools. This led to opportunities for the students to share their work beyond Los Angeles. In 2008, Ms. Garcia and a Wilson High student named Isaac were flown to California's state capitol to participate in an education panel with former California State Senator Gloria Romero. On a panel with about six other high school youth, Isaac shared his group's research on the state of education and offered his own personal experiences as illustrations. Ms. Garcia recalls Isaac's nervousness but also his confidence in being selected to speak for the youth of his community. He felt valued and appreciated, but most of all, the adults in the audience listened to him. Isaac had been recommended to CYR by one of his social studies teachers, who said he had great potential but was shy and could use a program like CYR to help him develop both academically and socially. Isaac's growth over 2 years in the program was powerful. Isaac continued to grow from his participation in CYR, and making multimodal presentations was second nature to him by the time he graduated from Wilson. He became a leader in the Wilson group and gradually took charge among his peers, leading activities, planning the documentary filmmaking process, and initiating interviews and conversations with other youth.

In fall of 2009, all the students and staff of CYR flew to Denver, Colorado, to present their research at the annual meeting of the American Educational Research Association (AERA). For some of the students from Wilson, it was their first time flying and going out of state. This was a monumental event because it was the first time that students presented action research at a conference traditionally reserved for adults. The Wilson students presented powerfully, with only limited support from Ms. Garcia, who simply advanced PowerPoint slides and cued up their digital video. They were so used to presenting that they were not anxious about an international education conference. Following their success at AERA, other opportunities for students to present came at their school, where they spoke to Wilson faculty at common planning time meetings, and the principal was always supportive and in attendance. Thus, this third space provided youth a way to access spaces, conversations, and knowledge typically reserved for adults. These students and their teachers created a respectful, challenging learning environment to discuss issues that directly affected their lives and those of their communities. They were introduced to new people, places, and dialogue; these experiences shaped their lives, and students over and over told us that they would never forget these experiences.

The student outcomes produced by the combination of critical pedagogy and critical media in the CYR group demonstrate the potential of third spaces. Academically, seeing students build their confidence over the school year and multiple years and find their voices among adult (and student) audiences was powerful. For students who were in the group multiple years, their presentation skills flourished, and their media literacy skills deepened. They needed less help making their videos and PowerPoint presentations—producing slides filled with media images, music, and video clips that showed deep analytical thinking. The students worked with technology that was much more complex than what their own schools offered, again showing that with guidance and resources, anything is possible, even for students whose intelligence and knowledge are often overlooked. Importantly, the students also became better advocates for themselves and the quality of education they were receiving at their school site. The students gradually started coming to Ms. Garcia and other supporters for help with difficult classes or strategies for handling conversations with teachers who held lower expectations of them or were not challenging them in class. This advocacy came from the students researching and learning the kinds of teaching they should be given every school day. A powerful transformation took place in these students' way of thinking about their education and the quality of the teaching, curriculum, and resources being provided to them. They realized that they deserved better and had the knowledge to support their concerns and the voice to make their demands.

Beyond academics and the development of knowledge in the field of education, CYR helped Ms. Garcia learn better ways of developing authentic relationships with students. It also helped students to develop powerful relationships with each other, another important outcome of critical teaching. Some of the CYR students came to the group with difficult life experiences, and the group provided support not just from a teacher but also from their peers. There were times when the students wanted to give up, not just because they were struggling in the group but also in their regular schooling due to personal circumstances. Other students had never committed to a group before and had to learn the value of working with others. The support of adults and peers, combined with the group's overall focus on giving a voice to young people and making change, ultimately kept the students motivated at the most difficult times. Ms. Garcia also learned not only about her students' interests and talents outside of school and their hopes and dreams, but also, and more importantly, the ways that students need adult support and mentorship. Ms. Garcia had many conversations about college and future goals with students, in part because all of the students she worked with would be first-generation college students. Most of them had very little knowledge about the college process, and the time they spent together to share information was invaluable. Most teachers desire and appreciate small classrooms so that they can really get to know their students, and the CYR group provided that environment. Ms. Garcia developed strong relationships not only with the students, but also with their families. Many of the parents expressed gratitude and appreciation for the support and time Ms. Garcia spent with the students, but also recognized the contribution of the entire UCLA program staff. During one of the summers, a student's mother invited the group over for lunch after a day of filming and interviewing and made homemade Mexican food. This provided an opportunity to chat with the parents and understand their hopes and dreams for their son. Other CYR parents would discuss their questions about their children's college future with Ms. Garcia and raise any other concerns they had or ask for advice about how to better support their son or daughter in the group. The opportunity to get to know parents at a closer level contributed to the progress of the group. These experiences in a different "classroom" environment provided by CYR deepened the importance of student–teacher and teacher–family relationships that translated into even stronger relationships with all of Ms. Garcia's students and families. The opportunity to work with students in a different context and structure can provide a real benefit not just to students, but also to teachers as they improve their own skills and practices so that the efforts toward encouragement, high expectations, and relationship building are continually renewed.

ART AND SOCIAL CHANGE AT ROOSEVELT

Roosevelt High School in Boyle Heights has a rich tradition of providing its students with opportunities to become engaged in third spaces. What makes the experience very powerful in these third spaces is that many school clubs have the mission to increase student civic engagement and develop values in social justice, community care, and love. Roosevelt High has a long history of community engagement, demonstrating a culture of resistance that dates back to the 1940s and characterized by radical Jewish youth clubs, community organizing against the 1954 "Operation Wetback," the student walkouts of the late 1960s, and students' continuing involvement in both the Chicano movement and the immigrant rights struggle (Villa & Sanchez, 2005). Students at Roosevelt have always been at the forefront of movements of resistance that address unjust wars and laws and overcrowded schools and demand ethnic studies classes, educational justice and equitable school conditions, and an end to the criminalization of youth. Students at Roosevelt have been involved and continue to be involved with organizations, clubs, and programs in Los Angeles and in Boyle Heights. When organizing the 1968 student walkouts to ensure higher rates of acceptance to local universities for students from the Eastside, students throughout the Eastside would often meet in a community space across the street from Roosevelt High. Boyle Heights is filled with third spaces of youth empowerment; some meetings take place in classrooms after school or during lunch, while others are in community centers and spaces, such as Primera Taza Café, Self-Help Graphics, Casa 0101, Corazon del Pueblo, or InnerCity Struggle.

Political education, self-expression, identity building, knowledge of self, and consciousness building take shape weekly on campus during lunch and after-school clubs. Taking Action is a student-led club of the Community Rights Campaign (CRC), a larger organization that addresses the criminalization of youth in Los Angeles and the school-to-prison pipeline. Taking Action youth meet weekly to learn through political education workshops and civic literacy, organizing skills in leading rallies and speaking to media and local leaders. Youth also learn how to use spoken-word, popular theater, and art installations as a tool to express youth concerns. Taking Action and the CRC led a successful campaign in building allies to challenge Los Angeles Municipal Code (LAMC) Section 45.04 that for year gave the Los Angeles Police Department the power to stop and cite students arriving late to school. The code was abused by police, who ticketed more than 47,000 LAUSD students at disproportionate rates, mostly targeting black and brown youth from low-income communities. Citations ranged from $240 for the first citation to more than $900 for the third, creating economic distress for families who were already struggling economically. As a result of this unjust law, many youth were criminalized, handcuffed, insulted, and sent to the juvenile courts, forcing them to miss school and emotionally affecting students by pushing them toward the jail track.

Passionate young people with a love for justice and a desire to create caring school conditions organized and gave it their all to change the unjust law. Students celebrated success along the way (increasing volunteers, gaining media recognition, having conversations with law enforcement, engaging in civic actions, etc.) as they neared amendment of the law. Youth celebrated with other youth nationally to express voices of struggle through a Virtual Rally, where students discussed their goals and victories via video conferencing. Young people discussed how the school-to-prison pipeline takes form in their respective schools. Cinthia Gonzalez, the Taking Action student leader and organizer at Roosevelt High, began with an opening statement where she passionately described the work of youth in Los Angeles:

> As youth we have a big duty in the movement to end the school to prison pipeline and to fend off the criminalization of black and brown people in the US. I have seen firsthand as an organizer. We have youth at Roosevelt

who have collected petitions, conducted rallies, and organized to fight for the end of truancy tickets. Our actions have a tremendous impact in winning fights. The work we do is local, but local can spread throughout the state, country, and globe. I'm stating that youth have the power to change things. The unity of youth can be combined with adults and we can all in solidarity create better changes for our community.

Youth from Taking Action received a great deal of media coverage in Los Angeles during their campaign and used multiple forms of media to publicize their campaign and successes. Students appeared on local news channels and in newspapers, such as Univision, the *Los Angeles Times*, and National Public Radio (NPR). Taking Action youth also produced their own critical media videos and articles that were shared with the public through the organization's webpage, YouTube, the school newspaper, and the *Boyle Heights Beat*, a community newspaper written by youth in collaboration with *La Opinion*, a local Spanish-language newspaper, and the University of Southern California Annenberg School of Journalism.

Taking Action effectively employed critical media pedagogy, and as a result, young people from Boyle Heights became critical of issues that affected their community, addressing poverty, criminalization, discrimination, and institutionalized racism. With their political consciousness, youth learned to organize using multiple forms of creative media and producing knowledge to raise awareness in youth and community members. Their work should be celebrated because it has become a model of effective youth organizing in achieving change. In February 2012, the campaign ended in a win for youth organizers, who, through coalition building, got the Los Angeles City Council to change the Daytime Curfew Law. After the affirmative vote, youth and organizers stood holding hands outside City Hall, chanting the words of Assata Shakur in a celebration of power: "It is *our* duty to fight for *our* freedom. It is *our* duty to win. *We* must love each other and support each other. *We* have *nothing to lose but our chains.*" Under the new law, rather than ticketing students who arrive late to school, the city of Los Angeles will have to provide resources and interventions to students in need, while creating a more supportive and caring school community for young people. A documentary that covers this successful campaign of youth power will soon be released.

Club students at Roosevelt use critical multimedia tools to engage other youth in their struggle and goals. The Dreamer's Club, an undocumented student support group, created patches that read "Support Dreamers" and "Support Undocumented Students." They collaborated with the ART Club to cut stencils and spray-paint the messages onto the patches. The club set up a table during lunch, and students lined up to get their patches of support pinned onto their backpacks. The club also distributed fliers promoting their meetings and providing information on assembly bills AB 130 and AB 131 that California Governor Jerry Brown had just signed, which qualify undocumented college students to receive financial aid and scholarships. Students walk around campus with their patches affixed to their book bags, which also include club pins made by the ART Club, United Students, and Taking Action.

The ART Club—which is acronym for Art of Revolutionary Teens— is a club that started at Roosevelt High in 2009 when Mr. López came across three students who had just received a small grant and wanted to use it to paint a mural, incorporating elements of urban graffiti art style. Students made fliers to distribute to their friends. Mr. López soon found that the Salesian Boys and Girls Club in Boyle Heights was offering grants to begin after-school programs for community youth. Mr. López and the students began to plan out their mural project idea and decided that it would be great to take it a step further and begin an after-school urban art club supported by funds from the Salesian Boys and Girls Club to maintain the program. Membership grew quickly, and many talented young artists and students interested in the arts began to attend the weekly meetings. Mr. López, having a love for the arts and knowing the positive power art has in the lives of youth, wanted to support students. He had just completed a service-learning project at Roosevelt High with the support of his partnership with the César E. Chavez Foundation, a non-profit organization that works with schools to create high-quality projects of this nature. This project brought indigenous human rights activist and Nobel Laureate Rigoberta Menchu Tum to the mural unveiling event to speak to youth. The event coincided with PeaceJam Global Call to Action, a 3-day event that brings together Nobel Peace Prize winners to celebrate youth civic engagement and projects that promote justice and peace. Roosevelt High hosted youth throughout the city and other states to paint a mural that promotes peace, justice, and youth activism.

Once the ART Club was up and running, Mr. López and the students began to plan the next mural project at Roosevelt High, which was to be an extension of the first mural project. Prominent community artist Raul Gonzalez from Mictlan Murals sat down with ART Club youth to design the images and message of the mural. Murals are public art, and the first step is to develop the social themes that the images will convey to the young people of the community as they walk by the mural. The first mural included images of indigenous people to acknowledge the communities' indigenous history and build pride, as well as depictions of young people marching in protest for youth rights, the Dream Act, and educational justice. ART Club members also wanted to include images of young people learning and of conscious-raising books, along with images of nature to lift consciousness about the importance of caring for "mother earth." The mural also includes the phrases "Si Se Puede," "Arte es Vida," "Resist," and "Knowledge of Self"—all done in graffiti art lettering, a style of art that young people feel connected to. The size, colors, images, and lettering together reflect the cultural identity of Boyle Heights youth and their experiences growing up in Los Angeles. The mural projects each contain multiple themes and messages that invite inquiry and curiosity from observers. Placing empowering murals on the walls of a school invites the community to learn from the knowledge produced by youth and artists and advocates for members of the Chicano/Latino community. It is important to engage youth members of the community in the mural development and painting process, which makes mural literacy richer and builds a closer personal relationship with the piece of art that students produce. Mural analysis and literacy skills are key; just as important are the mural production process skills, because they help young people become independent and confident in using public art as a tool for community empowerment. Art and murals can be a pedagogical tool for critical consciousness and identity building that flows out beyond the classroom and creates a permanent learning media on the walls of a community space. The process of painting a mural builds unity, art skills, knowledge, and responsibility for community beautification among community members. Politically and socially conscious murals build critical literacy in the participants and also in the community due to their nature as large-media production pieces. Murals have a long history as critical literacy tools in Latin America. After the Mexican Revolution, artists such as Diego Rivera, Clemente Orozco, and David Alfaro Siqueiros used mural media to build critical literacy among a large illiterate population that had been denied education by the ruling class. These great artists painted images dealing with themes of oppression, liberation, rebellion, and the celebration of their

Student Jennifer Castillo writing her poem on the mural project led
by artist Raul Gonzalez

indigenous culture and history. Similarly, 100 years later, community
artists and youth in Los Angeles continued to use the same media tool
to express similar themes, building critical literacy and empowering
community members.

The ART Club found it equally important to paint murals inside
Roosevelt High School, seeing that the school lacked murals that
addressed the historical experience and culture of the youth who attend the school. Every year, the mayor of Los Angeles carries out a
Mayor's Day of Service, where he encourages community members
to participate in beautifying Los Angeles through repainting walls
and planting trees and gardens. Mr. López advocated funding a mural project at Roosevelt High; his proposal to the City of Los Angeles
was accepted, and the next project began. He successfully replicated
the same approach to painting murals through writing proposals and
grants, leading to multiple mural projects inside Roosevelt High and a
well-funded after-school arts program. His successes prove that educators play a key role in being advocates for community resources and
serving as a bridge to channel city resources into their schools. Boyle
Heights is a community rich in cultural and social capital, filled with

talented artists, but it sometimes lacks the funding to roll out large projects. Mr. López is currently working with youth and artist Raul Gonzalez on two murals that will stand between a school's organic vegetable and medicinal gardens. The murals will promote community health and ancestral connection to the earth. Mr. López has also secured funding for a community oral history project that will use images to document and inform viewers about the long history of Boyle Heights. The project was made possible through a grant from UCLA's Teacher-Initiated Inquiry Projects (TIIP). Mr. López and a team of teachers wrote the grant to build critical social literacy and community activism. According to Clara Herrera, an ART Club member, "the art club allows us to express ourselves creatively . . . . [W]e can use art to make revolution and positive change." In an era where students are inundated with standardized tests in schools, both time and funding for the arts have been chipped away, creating a void in a critical part of educational development. Mr. López believes that the arts are crucial in building youth identity through human artistic expression and community building—a humanizing act in a dehumanizing era.

Students at Roosevelt High now walk into a historic school building with decorated walls that address their community's history of struggle and resistance and empower young people with images of youth protesting and engaging in direct action to secure ethnic studies and educational justice. Wenceslao Quiroz, a talented community artist from Boyle Heights who was once a student at Roosevelt, worked on a mural project with students at the high school. Wenceslao's schooling experience at Roosevelt was not positive; painting a mural on campus with youth who attended the school became a transformative act for him, leaving a permanent piece of empowering art that will speak to generations of youth. The mural Wenceslao led was part of a larger service event at Roosevelt High, the first annual Harvey Milk Day of Service, during which two campus vegetable gardens were installed. The design of the mural was generated by Roosevelt student members of the ART club, Taking Action, Student Voices, and the Gay Straight Alliance. The final design was a social and political mural that cut across history and included images of the Mexican Revolution, Zoot Suit riots, 1968 walkouts, Harvey Milk, and the Arizona student struggle for Ethnic/Chicano/a Studies. At the top center of the mural with her arms stretched is mother earth, represented as Ramona, a Zapatista indigenous leader from Chiapas, Mexico. On the Harvey Milk Day of Service, members of non-profit organizations volunteered to paint the mural and install two school gardens. Artist Wenceslao Quiroz gave the mayor of Los Angeles, Antonio Villaraigosa, who was in attendance, an explanation of the meaning and importance behind the images depicted on the mural. On the mural unveiling event, club students, Mr. López, and community artist Ramiro Hernandez shared spoken-word poetry, reflecting on the social/political consciousness behind the mural.

Political and socially grounded student clubs at Roosevelt created spaces that counter the marginalization that many students in Boyle Heights often face. Young people who participate in these *critical third space* clubs find a liberating experience and grow empowered and knowledgeable about oppressive societal institutions. Cooper and Huh (2008) define a *critical third space* as a metaphorical space of empowerment and transformation, where students learn to harness social and political capital. Educators, artists, and organizers who are guided by critical pedagogy, transformative praxis, and revolutionary love guide the club's students in critical inquiry and political art. Critical media pedagogy is embodied in club spaces, where students learn to be critical of institutions and systems of oppression and learn the skills to produce

Harvey Milk Day of Service Mural Project led by artist Wenceslao Quiroz

knowledge to better their world, using art and organizing tools. Third spaces play a crucial role in schools because, many times, they become the praxis behind the critical theory and knowledge learned in classrooms where educators are infusing their lessons with critical pedagogy. Young people who become critical of unjust institutions are eager to civically participate and engage in social change. Third spaces provide students with valuable experiences where they can flourish as critical pedagogues, while building deep relationships among youth leaders and radical adults. Learning organizing skills and using multiple forms of media tools make them effective agents of change, who can independently create community knowledge and become effective communicators who can counter marginalization and build a more just Los Angeles.

POWERFUL LITERACY THROUGH YOUTH DOCUMENTARY FILMMAKING

The title of the 8-minute student-created video is "Schooled on Watts," and it is being debuted at Los Angeles City Hall as part of the final presentations of the summer seminar. Over the course of 5 weeks, the high school student team, along with their teacher leader and a college undergraduate mentor who had been a member of the Council, have collected interviews, visited school sites, researched legislation, engaged state leaders, and consolidated the results and other materials that they have collected into a video that takes a critical view of spaces for the development of youth civic agency in California schools. The group is known for their catchy hip hop intros and fast-flowing montages of imagery from their beloved Watts, and the crowd of youth, teachers, educational leaders, parents, and elected officials sits in silent anticipation as the video is played. The Watts group does not disappoint.

The opening sequence begins with a still shot of the filmmakers with raised fists superimposed over a background with a Gorilla, a red star, and a title that reads "Guerilla Force Five: Flying Fists of Fury." Immediately, we are transitioned into a map of Watts and a voiceover from one of the student filmmakers who will serve as our narrator. She states, "Watts is known historically by the media for the Watts riots, notorious gang activity, low socioeconomic status, and currently its black and brown tensions, its violence, and its underperforming schools." As T-Pain's "All of the Above" booms in the background, the video takes us through a series of still shots and camera pans through apartment buildings, neighborhood shops, street signs, and newspaper clips of the infamous 1960s Watts riots. T-Pain's lyrics in this sequence include "I've done been through the pain and the sorrow/The struggle it's nothin but love (Nothin but love)/I'm a soldier a rider a ghetto survivor and all the above." As the opening sequence culminates, the voice of an older woman says, "Poor people always get everything last," followed by the sound of a jail cell clanging shut. The remaining 8 minutes contain a mix of interviews with elementary and secondary students and conversations with parents, teachers, and school and community leaders. It also includes data on achievement and the ongoing debates surrounding the shift to charter schools in South Los Angeles. The narrative is one of challenges and hope. In the final sequence, short clips feature students begging the system to support the needy and not the greedy. An older woman laments as she says, "I just pray it gets better!" An excited teacher exclaims, "People need to organize!"

In the final voiceover, our teen narrator concludes, "Historically marginalized? Disenfranchised beyond all hope? Are people afraid to dispel media stereotypes because of the truth they'll find or is it just too uncomfortable to realize Watts' potential? Watts youth are beautiful, creative, intellectual, full of power beyond society's expectations and can no longer be given up on because you've been schooled on Watts!" In a final touch that is nothing short of genius, each student filmmaker is featured engaged in some mundane, yet humorous activity such as pretending to trip walking up stairs, getting surprised coming out of a bathroom stall, break dancing, and doing cartwheels down the school hallway.

The Council of Youth Research (or CYR) has been working in Los Angeles for 12 years with students and teachers on the project of participatory action research, where young people develop research skills that allow them to collect, analyze, and present data about the educational conditions in urban America. For the past 7 years, this work has included the production and distribution of digital videos. We looked at data gathered from six summer seminars that produced digital video documentaries (2003, 2004, 2007, 2008, 2009, and 2010) to understand the intersection of traditional academic literacies and new media education. In addition to the five seminars, there were five Public Service Announcements (PSAs), each produced during the 2008–2009 and 2009–2010 academic years, for a total of 36 short videos that comprise the data set.

We will look at the production and distribution of these short videos in the context of recognizing the current goals of adolescent secondary literacy education. We want to illustrate that it is possible to have a literacy pedagogy that acknowledges the changing nature of literacy praxis while also acknowledging the continued need to help students acquire basic academic reading and writing skills. Another goal is to bring to bear empirical data to discuss the academic merit of critical media pedagogy. In focusing on youth media production in the context of the Council of Youth Research, we are interested in the following:

1. What are the basic, critical, and new media literacy practices that accompany the production of a short documentary film by urban adolescents?
2. How do youth distribute their media products? What civic and literacy skills are involved in the act of youth media distribution?
3. What are the prospects for youth media production in core content area classes in secondary classrooms?

However, before proceeding to a discussion of the "what," or the production of the digital videos, we want to briefly outline the conceptualization of what some call critical media pedagogy. In our work with the Youth Council, we were not only concerned with what was taught, but how it was taught. With respect to the production of media, we wanted youth to see themselves not only as producers of media, but as critical producers of media. This critical production can only emanate from a *critical media pedagogy*, or one that is both humanizing and problem-posing, while encouraging youth to engage their surroundings more powerfully as shapers of discourse and as agents of change.

CRITICAL MEDIA PEDAGOGY IN THE COUNCIL OF YOUTH RESEARCH

The larger research project of the Youth Council is guided by design experiment methodology, youth participatory action research (YPAR), new literacy studies, and, more recently, visual sociology. Through a design experiment methodology, the adult teachers and researchers draw upon the work of Brown (1992) and Palinscar (1995) to systematically analyze an intentionally created phenomenon, the Council of Youth Research, as an intervention designed to increase academic literacy and civic agency. Toward this goal, Mr. Morrell and the IDEA team of teachers and graduate students collect data on student identity development, student college-going, and student literacy development, as measured through an analysis of student work products. Additionally, the Youth Council is interested in the project of participatory action research, so the work is conducted collaboratively *with* students and communities, rather than *on* students and communities. These ideas about participatory action research are guided by the work of scholars who advocate for research methodologies that engage participants as collaborators and not just the objects of the researchers' gaze. Additionally, participatory action research is defined by whom it engages (marginalized publics), how it engages (collective activity), and why it engages (social transformation) (Kincheloe & McLaren, 1998; McIntyre, 2000; Morrell, 2008).

The Youth Council enables city youth to become powerful civic agents who create and disseminate knowledge about problems they care about. The Youth Council members are students from five Los Angeles high schools. These students examine and report on central questions affecting the lives of Los Angeles Unified School District (LAUSD) students. The members of the Youth Council study relevant literature on these questions and employ social science research methods to gather data in their schools and communities. They survey youth, observe classrooms, examine data collected by the district, interview public officials, and much more. The students regularly report their research findings to members of the media, elected state officials, the mayor's office, the school board, community-based organizations, students and educators at local schools, and the general public. Additionally, the students distribute their findings more widely via social media such as Facebook, YouTube, and Ning and via their blog and presentations to national research bodies.

Each year, the Council of Youth Research is comprised of approximately 30 students from across 5 comprehensive high schools in urban Los Angeles. Generally, each school furnishes a cohort of five to six students as well as a lead teacher who works with the students throughout the project. The schools are chosen from areas of the city that have traditionally been underserved: East Los Angeles, South Central Los Angeles, Downtown Los Angeles, and Watts. These schools include Roosevelt, Wilson, Manual Arts, Crenshaw, and Locke high schools. Teachers and administrators were selected for their dedication to the idea of the Youth Council.

Originally, the Institute for Democracy, Education, and Access (IDEA) faculty identified a lead teacher at each high school who had a demonstrated commitment to educating youth for engaged citizenship. Each of the teachers worked with the institute throughout the 3-year period of 2010–2012. Mr. Morrell and IDEA staff worked with the teachers to select and recruit cohorts of five to six students from the classes of 2010, 2011, and 2012 to participate. Once students graduate from the program, the teachers, in consultation with the program coordinator, select a new generation to replace the graduates. The goal is to identify students who are interested in working with others to improve the conditions of their schools. While students' interest in the project is the dominant criterion, IDEA staff also took steps to ensure that the cohorts reflected the gender, ethnic, socioeconomic, and achievement diversity of the schools they represented.

DOCUMENTARY VIDEO ANALYSIS

Part of teacher action research entails collecting information to determine whether and how students are learning. Mr. Morrell and the IDEA research team were interested in the powerful media literacies being developed through the process of documentary filmmaking, one of the Youth Council's key activities. Over the past decade, Mr. Morrell and the IDEA staff have amassed digital video footage of classroom interactions, digital video footage of student filmmakers, and digital photographs of the research and filmmaking processes. Over the 12 years of the seminar, they have amassed several thousand photographs. Mr. Morrell analyzed these photographs looking for shots that relate to any of the aspects of digital filmmaking (shooting, editing, etc.) and digital video footage of student presentations. Other sources of student work include group PowerPoint presentations, electronic versions of student journals, student essays, and student research reports ranging from 20 to 35 pages

To better understand the media literacy learning demonstrated in these videos, the IDEA team used a New Literacy Studies approach and looked for *literacy events,* or instances where student interactions were facilitated by traditional or multimodal literacy artifacts. Following the work of Heath (1982) and Barton and Hamilton (1998), they documented *literacy practices,* such as student participation in seminar discussions; students designing their research projects; students discussing existing research; students creating research instruments (i.e., interview protocols and surveys); students writing field notes while touring school sites, neighborhoods, and government offices; students taking photographs and capturing digital video footage; students analyzing data; students writing memos and research documents; students editing video footage; students creating PowerPoint slides; students writing notecards for their final presentations; and students rehearsing and delivering their final 20-minute research presentations.

They developed some deductive codes such as basic (academic) literacy events, which they defined in accordance with standards documents such as the Common Core State Standards (CCSS) and the NCTE/IRA Standards for English Language Arts. They also coded for critical literacy events and new media literacy events. The IDEA team realized early on that most of the existing research on ethnographies of communication focused either on print literacy or spoken language (Alim, 2006). They needed to theorize what method of analysis and which deductive codes made the most sense for a new media text like an iMovie. They explored filmmaking organizations (Director's Guild of America, Independent Film Organizations, Students and Professors at USC and UCLA, the Motion Picture Film Association, and International Documentary Association), as well as texts produced by these organizations, in order to develop a language to analyze the merit of new media production.

DIGITAL VIDEO PRODUCTION AND CRITICAL LITERACY IN THE YOUTH COUNCIL

Critical Literacy as Research Design and Data Collection

The students demonstrated a multitude of literacy skills as they designed and carried out the background research for each of their videos. While this took different forms for each group, there were many common elements. All students began with readings from educational research that explained the history of inequalities in schools. Some of these readings included work from Jean Anyon (1981) that explains how differently situated schools receive different forms of instruction. The students also read Angela Valenzuela's *Subtractive*

Schooling (1999), Paulo Freire's *Letters to Those Who Dare Teach* (2005), and Tara Yosso's "Community Cultural Wealth" (2005). They also read critical theorists like Antonio Gramsci, who explore concepts such as hegemony and explain how dominant societies use institutions such as school and the media to transmit messages that encourage marginalized groups to accept their subordination as normal and necessary. Gramsci (1971) identifies this process as *manufactured consent.* The work of these theorists becomes manifest in the students' textual production and informs their research design.

During the background research phase, the students are also collecting demographic data on their particular research sites. This includes exploring reports on the Department of Education website, looking at the Census Factfinder website, reviewing police reports, and reading a series of research reports on educational opportunity produced by the Institute for Democracy, Education, and Access (IDEA). At the same time, the students are developing their own tools to collect primary data, such as interviews and survey questions. Finally, they travel into the field, which for the seminar meant visiting neighborhoods, schools, community centers, homes, and the offices of elected officials. There, they talked with various stakeholders while shooting footage that would ultimately be edited into their final video documentaries.

Literacy Practices Involved in Filming, Editing, and Storyboarding

We also documented academic, critical, and new media literacies as the students filmed, edited, and storyboarded their digital videos. The students learned that whenever we traveled to a new location, they needed to gather video of the surrounding area to use as a backdrop in their films. This sort of filming is known as "B-roll footage" and is essential to transitions and establishing changes in location. Students became adept at figuring out what made the best B-roll footage (i.e., a sign welcoming them to a new city or neighborhood, the front entrance to a school or government office, street signs, etc.), and they knew to get both still shots and shots with the video cameras. Students also learned how to compose quality shots. As part of the media production curriculum in the seminar, the students learned how to compose tight shots (that leave little empty space), how to center the subject, and how to use tripods when necessary to avoid unnecessary shaking or blurriness. They also began to develop their own documentary style of shooting, which included panning through streets while driving a car slowly to get a feel for what it is like to walk down a block in their neighborhood. Finally, the students began to use their media lenses to find good locations to interview subjects for their documentary. Selecting a good location meant reading the light correctly and ideally finding some identifying markers in the backgrounds that made for interesting viewing.

Literacy Practices Associated with the Presentation of the Digital Videos

Students presented their videos in two ways. The public unveiling generally occurred as part of a public presentation. Over the life of the CYR this generally happened as

1. Part of a public forum at City Hall.
2. Part of a presentation at a state or national research conference.
3. Part of a meeting or a reception for the general public.

The second method of presentation generally happened in cyberspace through a website or other social media outlet such as YouTube or Facebook. With respect to the in-person presentations, youth would usually situate the viewing of the film within their more in-depth presentation of their research, so literacy practices included writing up the final research report, preparing the accompanying PowerPoint presentation, and scripting an introduction to the actual video. Each of the student groups usually writes out a 1-minute introduction that frames the film for the audience. The introductions include background information on how the film was made, who was involved in the making of the film, and what messages they, as filmmakers, would like the film to convey.

The second form of presentation involves preparing the film for virtual consumption. Students need to know which virtual outlets make the most sense to showcase, which formats to save the film in to make it easy to upload onto the various social media sites, and how to "market" their films via social media. Once the films are uploaded onto websites such as YouTube, the students begin embedding the links to the film on their own social media pages. This is normally accompanied by some sort of written message to their friends and followers, many of whom will be tagged in a post that encourages them to watch and disseminate the film widely. The filmmakers also field questions and comments made by viewers through the dialogue function that most of these sites have. It is not unusual to see several dozen comments from viewers and to have all of these responses commented upon by the high school filmmakers.

Critical Literacy as the Distribution of Digital Video Texts

Critical media literacy also entails having the skills to distribute a text. How are youth autonomously distributing their videotexts? We began talking about distribution in the previous section, but to illuminate this process further, we offer a specific example—namely, the Educational Leadership group, which created a 7-minute documentary for the August 2010 presentation. However, at the conclusion of the seminar, the group still felt as though their documentary was not finished. Two weeks later, they posted a more finalized 10-minute version of the documentary on Facebook. This is evidence of the youth using mechanisms of distribution that are familiar to them. Here is a short list of multiple spaces where the youth videos have been distributed:

- The Facebook pages of individual students, of the institute, and of teachers and faculty.
- The youths' blog, entitled "Young Critical Minds," which disseminates the work of the Youth Council. A few of the student groups have also used their filmmaking capabilities to produce video blogs to accompany their written texts.
- YouTube pages created by institute faculty and by teachers.
- Ning.com sites created by teachers.
- The Institute for Democracy, Education, and Access (IDEA) website.
- The website of New America media.
- A DVD that students sent out to the local and national media, teachers, educational leaders, congressional representatives, state legislators, philanthropic foundations, and university scholars.

CONCLUSION

While working with youth who are making documentary films holds tremendous promise for the field of literacy, there are some limitations of this teaching method. First, it is difficult to say how the summer model will translate into practice in 7 to 12 classrooms where teachers have limited time during class periods and many more demands on their time than teachers of a summer seminar. We also have a tremendous amount of resources in the summer component of our program, which includes access to technology and the help of undergraduate student volunteers that decreases our student-to-teacher ratio to 5:1. Further, the 6-week unit is relatively short compared to a full semester or year-long curriculum.

Additionally, there are no pre- and post-tests to say exactly how students gained in literacy skills. Nor was there specific follow-up to determine whether there was a jump in student academic performance when they returned to school in the following year. However, there are data on grades and college access, which point to the connection between participation in the work of the Youth Council and college access. But it is not possible to specifically identify one activity, such as the making of documentary films, as being responsible for that difference.

8   Conclusion

For educators, critical media curricula are not always readily available. That is why we need to visit bookstores and websites to search for material. I ordered many books on cultural studies, media, and hip hop, to educate myself and to find readings for class curricular use. The knowledge will be scattered and educators will need to find it, pull it together, think of themes, and construct meaningful lessons and units using their creativity, skills, and tools. We must reflect and think critically about issues that matter to young people to figure out how to put the material to use.

—Jorge López

My concern is that we fall in love with the media and forget about the critical pedagogy. The blogging, the digital filmmaking, the spoken-word poetry, and the use of visual media are all essential to the development of powerful literacies in the 21st century, but it all pales in comparison to the need to have powerful educators who understand youth's potential, who build real relationships with students, and who engage these youth in a participatory learning process that values their backgrounds and experiences and cultivates their intellectual energy in an environment that develops culturally sustained, self-actualized producers and disseminators of knowledge.

—Ernest Morrell

Engaging in critical media literacy curriculum with my students has made me a better teacher and person. I worked harder, was more reflective, and even took on a stronger identity as a civic agent myself. Most importantly, I learned how to really listen and learn from students. This effort to acknowledge them increased their confidence and allowed them to see themselves as intellectuals. We need more educators to dedicate themselves to working with students in a more critical and empowering way.

—Veronica Garcia

How can the narratives we've shared throughout these chapters of youth working powerfully through media illuminate possibilities for secondary humanities education at the dawn of the 21st century? How do teachers of English and social studies tap into this powerful and productive moment in communications technologies while also adhering to the disciplinary content standards? Do these standards need to be updated or modified, and if they do, what does that look like? How do the concepts and practices that we've associated with critical pedagogy manifest themselves in this new theory of humanities teaching? What kinds of skills and training are essential for new and experienced teachers to grasp and implement critical media literacy pedagogies? What roles do university-based teacher education programs and K–12 school sites play in supporting the study of critical media studies and critical teaching practices?

We were left with these questions and many more as we neared the completion of this text. Our initial goal was to offer as compelling and defensible a story as we could concerning the critical uses of media in secondary humanities classrooms, but in pulling together these narratives, we realized that there were larger implications for not only what to teach, but how we teach and, more importantly, how we position ourselves as educators in relation to these newly conceived youth intellectuals. In each of our meetings as an author team, we became involved in long conversations about the nature of teaching, about the state of schools, and about the untapped power of young people. Much of the substance of these conversations did not fit narrowly into the structure of the book's chapters, which understandably focus on curriculum design, implementation, and evaluation of student learning. However, we knew that we did not want to conclude the book without talking about teachers, powerful teaching, and the repositioning of youth as intellectuals, cultural producers, and civic agents.

To begin, we want to conclude with a strong statement about the importance of the terms *critical* and *pedagogy* to contextualize the focus on youth media engagement. Too often, we feel, curricular interventions focus on the "what" of teaching to the exclusion of the "how" or "why" aspects of pedagogy. That, we feel, is a tragic mistake. Also, we wanted to preemptively address legitimate concerns from our colleagues who may feel under-resourced, under-prepared, or under-authorized to enact this sort of media pedagogy in their classrooms, even if it does sound appealing.

One goal, then, in this final chapter is to show that even teachers with minimal instincts regarding new media literacies can bring them into classrooms in powerful ways. We say this as a group of teachers who all fit into this category! We also want to show that it is possible to think about infusing critical media education into all facets of the traditional secondary humanities curricula without losing our focus on academic literacy development or disciplinary content knowledge. Finally, we want to reaffirm our commitment to *critical pedagogy,* a model of empowering teaching that humanizes youth as it also sets high expectations and develops much-needed competencies for postsecondary education, for life, and for civic engagement in the 21st century. Toward these ends, we speak to the need for building relationships and developing meta-narratives of schools as potential sites of either social reproduction or social change. No technological tools, in and of themselves, will lead to change in city schools. That change will only come through teachers who draw upon these critical frameworks to create learning communities where the use of media tools becomes an empowering enterprise.

A FINAL WORD ON CRITICAL TEACHING

Critical pedagogy is often maligned for being too "academic" or theoretical, but its message to us as educators has been clear, and its importance to how we have framed our approach to teaching cannot be overstated. When we think about teaching critically, we think about how teachers relate to students, how they relate to the profession, and how they challenge current injustices in schools and society. With respect to the former, we as educators must have a truly deep love for this profession and the students we serve no matter who they are; it takes this kind of unconditional love to embrace the journey of critical pedagogy with our students, regardless of the media studies. This is about how we teach, for what purpose we teach, and how we advocate for and with our students. We understand that it is controversial to talk about love in the context of teaching, but that doesn't make it unnecessary. Mr. Morrell and a colleague (Duncan-Andrade & Morrell, 2008) challenged educators to frame their work in the context of love once before, but we thought we would conclude by offering some specific examples of how this love might manifest itself in critical pedagogy.

First, having a love for students means a love for the potential of all students. More tragic than the rampant failure we see in schools and classrooms are the expectation of failure and the acceptance of failure. It is difficult to hold low expectations for those you love. Three of the four of us are parents, and we have all collectively taught thousands of youth. It is difficult for us to accept that any of them will not succeed academically. Yet we understand that we are operating against a set of social norms that plans for the failure of a significant number of our students. At the same time, we witness the results of powerful teaching all across the nation. If powerful teaching is an intervention that changes the trajectories of students and schools daily, then educational failure cannot be solely or primarily attributable to the students.

One way this love translates specifically into critical pedagogy is through making meaningful connections to students and constantly affirming their potential. We know from attachment theory (Selman, 2003) that young people need to form meaningful attachments with their caretakers and mentors if they are going to establish the trust they need to truly grow and develop. This care is not an extra, and it is not soft; rather, it is actually necessary in many cases for the transaction of learning, especially among youth. Young people also respond to positive encouragement that is reinforced by actual progress. It is difficult to continue encouraging students if we haven't created the opportunities for them to experience success in our classrooms. The units described in these chapters discuss the attention to students' identities that the teachers made a point of addressing in their classrooms. The success of their work with students is a result of making those connections and affirming students right from the start of the school year. These efforts are essential for positive and caring student–teacher relationships and successful academic outcomes.

In addition to experiencing academic success, educational scholars have emphasized the importance of promoting cultural competence (Ladson-Billings, 1994) or self-actualization (hooks, 1994). Over the past decade, we have moved away from these foci in response to high-stakes examinations and core standards. While these may be necessary components of our educational system, they do not negate the need to build self-esteem, positive academic self-concept, worth, cultural affirmation, and pride in our students. Even further, education has been connected to the nurturing of future citizens for more than 2500 years in Western civilization.

A manifestation of love, then, is to continue to humanize the learning environment in ways that help students to feel good about themselves as learners and as people. The work of Claude Steele and his colleague Joshua Aronson (1995) points to the negative impacts of *stereotype threat* on students in high-stakes situations. Often, the threat is associated with feelings of inferiority based on race, gender, or perceived ability. As educators, we have the power to increase stereotype threat, but we can also minimize it through a focus on empowered academic identity development for our students. While curricula may benefit this process, it more importantly comes down to the art of teaching.

Critical teaching is also concerned with the nature of learning in classrooms and not just the content of the learning. In addition to having dynamic curricula that tap into the lived experiences of our students, we also need to complement those powerful curricula with powerful approaches to teaching. Paulo Freire (1970), for example, was very critical of a "banking" educational system where knowledge was disseminated to students in a hierarchical and ultimately silencing manner. In contrast to these approaches, which neither engage students nor honor their voices, Freire advocates for placing generative and productive dialogue at the center of the learning enterprise. We couldn't agree more. A critical teaching should be liberating for the students in that it gives them a freedom to express themselves and to contribute to the production of knowledge in the classroom. The examples we have shown attempt to go one step further. Not only do we want students to add to the knowledge of the classroom, we also feel that students can use the products they create in our classes to engage in a productive and generative dialogue with the general public. Whenever possible, we advocate creating spaces for students to share their work with peers from other classes, teachers and staff, parents, and the larger community. This promise provides an authentic context and purpose to the enterprise of textual production and affirms the students as intellectuals and active civic agents. Of course, this is not possible with every assignment, but we argue that more spaces for shared dialogue have a legitimate place in the curriculum.

Finally, as teachers, we also need to be critically reflective about who we are and our beliefs and ideas about education and young people because they shape what is done in the classroom. Incorporating social issues into standards-based content areas is not impossible, but it takes a concerted effort by teachers to draw out and make connections. As critical teachers, we must be aware not just of local issues, but also of national and international events and topics shaping the world and our students' lives, either directly or indirectly. Students also come into our classrooms with knowledge about important events and we must be skilled enough and feel encouraged to draw upon their knowledge for classroom learning. Units can be designed with overarching essential questions that encourage youth to be inquisitive about social issues and themes that can be applied throughout history and many world societies. Teachers who manifest love in the classroom typically create curriculum while keeping in mind how it will empower and better the lives of both students and the local and global community they see themselves as a part of. Not only do students benefit, but teachers also become more connected to the students and the surrounding school community. It is this inclusive and productive Freirian dialogue that honors the voice of students and facilitates them in learning academic content and academic literacy skills. We now briefly turn to a discussion of implications of our work for rethinking English and social studies education.

RETHINKING ENGLISH INSTRUCTION

Rather than think about media studies as a separate content area, we need to push for the inclusion of media literacies within the discipline of English. This is already beginning to happen at colleges and universities, where English majors are studying music, films, and cyberspace in their courses. Additionally, in digital rhetoric courses, young people are learning about design as they produce websites, blogs, and short films as assignments. Robert Scholes, in *The Rise and Fall of English: Reconstructing English as a Discipline* (1999), predicts that the future of English will involve more attention to new media textuality. We should not be afraid of the change, nor should we be alarmed. Language instruction has always changed with the advent of new technologies. Several centuries ago, students would have largely been focused on the rules of debate and the principles of speech in what would have been called Rhetoric courses. Only within the last 150 years have students have been focused on the study of literary texts in *English* rather than in classes centered on the study of classical Greek and Latin texts. Still more recently, we have become focused on students as writers, not just speakers or readers. Each of these changes has been important for the discipline to remain relevant in producing powerful and articulate citizens of the world. With this frame in mind, it only makes sense that the English classrooms of the 21st century will include the study and the production of multimodal texts.

While the focus within a content area such as English is heavily weighted toward standards-based ideas and instructional strategies, teachers can still incorporate student voices and critical media studies. The Common Core State Standards already include standards in each domain (reading, writing, and listening and speaking) that incorporate the use of media in the curriculum. These standards ask students to conduct research on various topics using the Internet, analyze the ways in which different mediums present information, and synthesize and present information using technology. These standards also challenge students to go further and even compare and contrast and evaluate media genres and presentations of sources of information, such as film or text. Although some of the media standards are written within a specific domain, some are more general and can be applied to any unit of study. The goal is to provide students with opportunities to learn, practice, and apply their knowledge of media literacies throughout their experience in the classroom, but also to show them how to be *critical* of the different forms of media as they engage with them.

Many students come into high school English classrooms with negative perceptions of this field based on their prior experiences with reading and writing. Teachers can liberate students' hearts and minds with an empowering curriculum, showing them that they can enjoy and learn in a powerful way. Students need opportunities to read texts that are culturally relevant and academically challenging, and they need to participate in learning communities that allow them to engage in higher-level conversations about critical issues within these texts. We need to hold our students to high expectations, guiding them through rigorous academic processes. English is a content area that translates to and is applicable to all others; the possibilities for a productive and engaging curriculum for students are endless. If students can learn to love the many kinds of elements and concepts within English, they can then apply their skills to other subjects. Reading, writing, and critical thinking are just some of the key skills for English, but incorporating popular culture and other media literacies within the classroom can help students engage with their other studies more deeply.

RETHINKING SOCIAL STUDIES

Teaching social studies should not become solely about the tested content, especially because of the current standardized-test-obsessed environment in education. The primary focus of education should not be confined to raising test scores, but should also include raising critical consciousness and civic engagement—and no discipline is more important to the latter than social studies. Social studies education in the 21st century should, in our estimation, have a stronger focus on the Freirean problem-posing approach to education, where students learn to care about problems and participate in activities to challenge injustices. Freire describes this as a revolutionary-humanist act; we believe that social studies teaching must be critical and that educators must understand the role of contributing to the humanizing of young people. It is imperative for social justice educators to understand that youth have power and that one of our most crucial roles as educators is facilitating this realization in youth. Social studies classrooms can become spaces where students learn frameworks of knowledge, examine theory, and learn how to make better sense of their world as young intellectuals. Youth can grow into confident intellectuals who master dialogue and learn to use language to advocate for their lives and their communities. It is necessary that critical pedagogy have a strong presence in social studies classrooms if educators want their students to understand the institutions of oppression that surround them and learn how to use tools of liberation.

Social studies courses can reveal the root causes of societal consequences and provide answers to unanswered questions in the lives of youth. Social studies classes, such as World and U.S. History, can offer multiple models of liberation and examples of successful struggles through history, which can serve to inspire young people and motivate them to become agents of change to better their lives and their communities. Critical media education can be viewed as a toolbox for social studies classrooms that teachers can use to empower young people with media skills to become producers of their own knowledge. Critical media education is a great fit in social studies courses that use project-based learning. The use of media tools can be interwoven through the project to further engage students and open up more possibilities to the project's outcomes. For example, Mr. López took his students on a field trip to the Occupy L.A. movement at City Hall. Students, broken up into teams of four, were assigned a camera and given the task of collecting voices and engaging in critical inquiry by asking questions about political and economic ideologies, civic engagement, and the mission of the Occupy movement. Students were inquisitive and engaged, capturing footage, taking photos, asking questions, and taking notes. Having the opportunity to connect through dialogue with people who are deeply committed to social change, and who have been disenfranchised by the economic system, became a meaningful learning experience for them. Unlike a textbook, students had the opportunity to visually see the movement and exchange words with these interview subjects. Taking on a journalist persona, students captured footage and prepared a presentation of their interviews. When reporting to their peers, students used their media videos and pictures to share their insights, impressions, and knowledge. We believe that social studies courses can contribute to the cultivation of a public intelligence that can push for progressive social change, in what John Dewey called a public sphere where citizens engage in participatory social inquiry to end social problems and inequalities (Oakes & Rogers, 2006).

These ideas, we believe, fit squarely within the mission of traditional social studies courses such as U.S. History, World History, and U.S. Government. However, we recognize that social studies, because of its content, is often viewed as overtly political, and any criticism of the United States' historical or contemporary role in oppressing others is viewed as anti-American. Similarly, any movements that demonstrate the achievements and activism of historically marginalized groups are also subject to extra scrutiny and even punishment. We say this in recognition of colleagues in Arizona who are no longer able to teach Mexican American Studies because the subject is understood as promoting hate. In resistance, educators and teacher activists throughout the nation have formed coalitions and are organizing to support teachers in Tucson, Arizona, by committing to teach Ethnic Studies in their classrooms; legally challenging the ban on Mexican American Studies; and demanding that banned, warehoused critical texts such as Paulo Freire's *Pedagogy of the Oppressed* (1970) and Rudolfo Acuña's *Occupied America* (1988) be returned to their classrooms.

This controversy only underscores our need to fundamentally rethink the approaches and tools that we use in social studies to understand how societies work and how inequity happens. We advocate teachers who involve students in the process of asking difficult questions and using media tools to unpack invisible ideologies that lead to different experiences within the same society. Youth can also use their media tools to promote new social knowledge that recasts marginalized communities differently, both historically and in the present. Mr. Morrell is currently working with colleagues in New York to enable students to tell different stories about the history of education in their community through traditional and new media avenues.

YOUTH MEDIA PRODUCTION IN THIRD SPACES

The success of media production with students at Wilson, Roosevelt, and across Los Angeles with the Council of Youth Research calls for educators to find ways of increasing and sustaining similar opportunities for students. There should be extracurricular spaces on campus that focus on media production, such as TV stations, online newspapers, radio stations, recording studios, and so forth. We must also think about audience and presentation in creating spaces for students to share their production with the world. Teachers can play a significant role in supporting student development of media in several ways. Students today may be more knowledgeable than teachers about media resources; teachers can work with students and use their knowledge as one starting point to produce media. Teachers can also start small projects before trying complex assignments involving media and then build that into the larger curriculum. Colleagues who are willing to collaborate and learn how to use media in their classrooms must seek out and form partnerships to work together. The backlash and fear that have resulted from the push for standards and standardized tests can be effectively countered by taking various actions. Educators must show exemplars of student work to other teachers and administrators and allow them to see how critical media production can be embedded in a standards-based curriculum (i.e., faculty meetings, department meetings, classroom observations and presentations). These educators can also provide spaces for students to present their work to other educators outside of school (i.e., conferences, public forums, community events). Assessment of these multimodal products can be done by building on, and revising, the current standards we have that address the use of media. In public education forums such as the National Council of Teachers of English (NCTE), the International Reading Association (IRA), and the National Council for the Social Studies (NCSS), educators can critically examine the work being done to embed media literacies in classrooms. Their action research projects can then lead to a discussion of how future revisions of content-based standards can further encourage and support student media production.

How do we give a larger purpose to the work that we have students create on our behalf? How do we link the production of media with the challenge of making education meaningful to the students while they are in our classrooms and schools? The Council of Youth Research continues to have an impact beyond their own schools—their students have traveled to the State Capitol and presented to packed audiences at national education conferences. They have gained access to powerful spaces and spoken with key educators and policymakers about their research and recommendations for change. The students' work at Wilson and Roosevelt has affected other teachers, administrators, and their local communities and schools. In order to continue to affect the lives of youth in these powerful ways, we must continue to share the work and get new teachers and more colleges and universities on board, exposing the role and success that media production can have for students.

MEDIA PRODUCTION, STANDARDS, AND POLICY IN HUMANITIES EDUCATION

Although we advocate here for substantial changes in literacy policy and content-area standards in English language arts and social studies to account for the age of participatory media, it would be inaccurate for us to suggest that the current standards do not address media learning. Both the Common Core State Standards and the LEARN Act address the changing nature of literacy and the need to incorporate media studies and media production into literacy education.

To produce powerfully literate college- and career-ready students in the 21st century, the Common Core State Standards have acknowledged the need to enable youth to interpret and create media. The California History-Social Science Framework supports the use of technology and media to "engage students actively in the learning process." The use of new media and technology is seen as an invaluable resource in teaching history, geography, economics, and other social science disciplines. According to the framework, teachers are expected to integrate history with other disciplines and collaborate with teachers in other fields. Its introduction makes a call to all educators, emphasizing their responsibility in preparing 21st-century children for the challenges of living in a fast-changing society. The National Council for Social Studies (NCSS), in its published national curriculum standards, asserts that the aim of social studies is the promotion of civic competence required of students to be active and engaged participants in public life. In 2009, the NCSS released the *NCSS Position Statement on Media Literacy*, recognizing the imperative role of social studies in a participatory democracy, highlighting the need to prepare students to critically question information and media in order to be better prepared to shape democracy for the public good. NCSS encourages a media education model built on critical inquiry to increase media literacy skills through social studies classrooms. Media literacy skills are embedded throughout its curriculum standards, which call for students to acquire "the ability to differentiate between primary and secondary sources or distinguish fact from fiction," an ability that "is now intimately connected to the ability to analyze and create media" (NCSS, 2009, n.p.). Participatory media education is needed in 21st-century social studies civic education. NCSS recognizes the changing role of technology and media and the need for a new pedagogy that empowers students to read and produce media in order to be active participants in our contemporary democracy.

During the second decade of the 21st century, we can no longer afford to consider media education as an add-on to a basic, standards-based curriculum. Students should be able to include their media products in digital portfolios that follow them throughout their educational years. There should be some place for these portfolios to be considered for K–12 admissions and higher education. In general, most measures of learning and summative evaluation do not incorporate enough real examples of student work. Nowhere is this more obvious than in the application process, whether for middle or high school, university, or competitive scholarships. We argue that there need to be more spaces for students to share their work as an example of their promise, and this work should include examples of media production. We think that colleges and universities, for example, should be able to take into consideration the PowerPoint slides and digital films created by the Council of Youth Research.

EQUIPPING SCHOOLS AND CLASSROOMS
FOR MEDIA PRODUCTION

The United States has a $15 trillion gross domestic product and a $3 trillion annual budget, yet we struggle to put iPads in the hands of our public-school children. This seems to me an issue of priorities more than it is an issue of available resources.

—Ernest Morrell

When Mr. Morrell asks his 4-year old son over dinner what one needs to become a successful musical artist, even he knows that the right technological tools are essential. It is not possible to have a rock band without the instruments and the knowledge to use them. The same can be said for schools and media production. Without equipping schools with the correct tools, we will not achieve our desired outcome. The obvious challenge is an economic one, but we argue that the real challenge is one of ideology and not economy. We have the means to fund schools in the ways that we, as a society, deem necessary and prudent. There are no shortages of security guards at urban secondary schools, and literacy curricular packages run in the thousands of dollars. In comparison, purchasing LCD projectors, laptops, tablets, and digital video cameras would involve relatively minimal expense. This type of investment won't happen without advocacy, though, on the part of the teachers, parents, students, and educational researchers who can levy data to support the inclusion of media production into instruction in the core content areas. Educators play a central role in advocating for classroom resources and media tools. Mr. López has used Donors Choose to gather art resources for his art club, and an HDTV to screen media in his classroom. Mr. López and a team of teachers from his school received a Teacher-Initiated Inquiry Projects (TIIP) grant from UCLA; with the grant they purchased cameras, laptops, and iMac stations for their classrooms. They also bought software, such as Final Cut Pro, for students to use in media production. The grant allowed teachers to attend training on using technology and new media with students to raise critical civic engagement. Mr. López took a documentary-making training class to teach his students how to produce their own videos. Their principal, Mr. Ben Gertner, has also been proactive in getting technology such as iPads and iPod carts in classrooms to build literacy and to use for media production. Principal Gertner and the School Site Council, on which Mr. López sits, have made it a priority to use school funds to purchase MacBook carts and technology for students to use. It is crucial for school faculty to be proactive in grant searching and writing and strategic in building partnerships with service providers to put technology in the hands of public-school students.

TEACHERS AS MEDIA PRODUCERS

As with any professionals whose industry has witnessed a massive change in technological capacity, teachers will need to learn on the job how to become media producers themselves if they want to create spaces in their classrooms for students to develop their media production skills. It is not enough simply to purchase the tools; they will also need to develop expertise. In most urban communities, community film centers exist that are open to youth and educators. In Boyle Heights, youth learn to make films at the Boyle Heights Technology Youth Center and *Centro de Comunicación Comunitaria* (Center for Community Communication). As mentioned earlier, Mr. López learned how to produce media by taking training in documentary making at the Echo Park Film Center, where he learned to produce and edit using Final Cut Pro. He created a short documentary, "Boyle Heights Youth Cultures of Resistance," which was viewed at a community-screening event. During the production process, Mr. López would often be seen conducting interviews, carrying a camera, and recording footage. Students asked why he was collecting video footage, and Mr. López would respond that he was learning to be able to better teach students how to produce their own videos. We believe that educators must model to their students the modalities of media intellectuals, which involves the engagement of media tools with youth and community members and the sharing of produced media through screenings and social media.

Following the National Writing Project model, it would be ideal to create more opportunities for teachers to learn how to shoot and edit their own films. Aside from thinking about content-area demands or incorporating media into standards-based curricula, teachers need time to just play around with the tools to understand their various uses. When our teachers become more comfortable with the process of media production, we'll see more of it in everyday classroom life.

MEDIA LITERACY ACROSS CONTENT AREAS

Although there may come a time when we do have courses in media production, we also need to think about media consumption and production as core literacies that need to be infused across the content areas. The examples shown in this book demonstrate only a small handful of the myriad ways that media studies can be incorporated into traditional secondary English and social studies curricula. There are also opportunities to include media studies in elementary classrooms, as well as math and science courses. Reading and "writing" media have to be envisioned as core competencies to be developed at each grade level and across all content areas if we are truly to have a media-literate America.

At some point, we are going to have to ask ourselves why we teach what we do in the ways that we do. However, that is beyond the scope of this book. We will say, though, that even though our approach has been pragmatic, it is also critical. Even as we fight to make transparent the logic of schooling, we have to intervene at the contemporary moment in day-to-day practices. What this means is that we may question the structure of the school day in secondary education and we may question the selection of English, social studies, science, and mathematics as core content areas. However, while we push at the logic and the limits, millions of young people are educated daily within these content areas, and we must figure out how to make the existing content areas engaging and accessible. Wherever we land in our ongoing conversation about the content areas that will be taught, we argue that media production can form a core competency that exists across content areas, much as reading and writing do now. Rather than focusing only on media studies as a content area, we have been advocating for media production as literacy—as a set of foundational skills with applications across all substantive areas of K–12 education. While we would like to see separate standards for media education, we would like for each grade level and discipline to contemplate how they would incorporate media into their core instruction.

THE IMPORTANCE OF HUMAN (AND HUMANE) RELATIONSHIPS

Even though the book is largely concerned with media production and developing tools to create and distribute new media products, the underlying pedagogy is still what makes the difference in quality teaching. Fancy tools such as tablets and flip-cams do not take the place of establishing meaningful relationships with students, demanding excellence from them, and believing in them. It is the daily doses of authentic caring and mutual respect that facilitate learning and empowerment.

Students need to be able to use the tools at their disposal to tell uncomfortable narratives about the world around them; they need trust and permission to be critical, to speak the truth to power, and to alter their relationship with the immediate world around them. Teachers need to be open to critical dialogue with students and comfortable discussing issues that may feel unfamiliar or uncomfortable; these can become powerful teaching moments. As student–teacher relationships develop as a result of the work, it is important for teachers to be prepared for the potential for students to open up about their lives. Over the years, in our experience with students and the work we do such as narratives, poetry, essays, or projects, students have opened up about serious issues they have experienced. In these extreme or rare instances, teachers may require some outside support and need to know when to seek help in supporting the student. The possibility of these delicate situations should not deter teachers from giving students the opportunity to have a voice in the classroom.

THE NEED FOR ADVOCACY (AND ADVOCATES)

Part of our theory of change asserts that educators must be advocates for the changes they want to see in classrooms and schools. We say this from our collective half-century of involvement in urban education. While the nation remains wealthy and drives the global economy, schools in inner cities and rural areas struggle to provide basic supplies for students. For the past 30 years, colleagues in our field have pointed to structural inequalities in schools that result in funding inequities (Kozol, 1991), tracking (Oakes, 1985), and curriculum that often fails to acknowledge the cultural diversity of America's classrooms (Banks, 1981; Ladson-Billings, 1995; Nieto & Bode, 2007). We mention these contexts because they affect our collective ability to implement many of the powerful practices that we've shared in this book. We still see many under-resourced schools and classrooms that lack access to appropriate technological tools, and we still see the effects of attitudes about social class and school knowledge (Anyon, 1981) that operate under limited belief about what working-class kids should be doing in school that affect the culture of schooling and students' attitudes about themselves. Finally, we live and work in a context where many teachers justifiably feel that classrooms are spaces that limit creativity for teachers and students. The current testing climate often takes precedence over focusing on activities that allow students to create and develop their voices via multimodal production. Again, these reductive practices are skewed toward schools and teachers that serve poorer students.

So, what does advocacy look like for busy classroom teachers given this context? One subtle way to advocate is to demonstrate the possibility of inserting media into standards-based units. The standards may represent the overall guiding lens to curriculum, but our collective experience suggests that they don't rule out room for creativity in the classroom; there are ways to incorporate engaging media-based lessons in every unit. Ultimately, though, in order to create spaces such as the ones described in this book, advocacy can take the form of classroom-based research in innovative practices, which forces a serious reconsideration of the road we have decided to follow in education reform. We over-test, we over-standardize, and we do not always treat students and teachers as intellectuals. However, the best way to make the case that we should do things differently is by shining a light on alternative practices that develop the same sorts of skills and abilities in more humane and culturally appropriate ways. One of the reasons we decided to write this book is that we want to add to current conversations about what constitutes effective classroom instruction. Though we want to be relevant and standards-based, we would cease to be critical if we did not remain fervently opposed to the current testing and standards regimes that dominate contemporary practice in schools. We side with John Dewey, Paulo Freire, and others who contend that kids learn best when pursuing their natural curiosity about the world around them.

Finally, advocacy means bringing continued attention to the reality that schools are not resourced in equal ways. We are writing this book during a time of severe economic crisis that disproportionally affects the students and the schools where this work takes place. The economic conditions affect the possibilities for powerful media production in some pretty obvious ways. Without sufficient budgets, schools are unable to access tablets, laptops, digital video cameras, and software packages that are needed to facilitate youth media production. Collectives of teachers, parents, and students can lobby state lawmakers and federal education officials to adequately fund schools to produce the citizens and workers that America needs. We have also witnessed on a smaller scale how teachers, as advocates for equitable resources, have secured funds via grants and fundraisers and strategic collaborations with universities and community-based organizations.

MEDIA LITERACY AS CIVIC ENGAGEMENT

Much is made of the uses of media in the world of work. Certainly, future generations will need to be media literate if they are to fit into the workplaces of the 21st century (Friedman, 2007). However, we also need to consider media literacies as central to the project of civic engagement. That is, if our students are to become full participants in civil society, they will have to be able to understand the media they inherit, but they will also need to be able to produce various genres of media to communicate with others locally and globally.

We need to theorize media as a core literacy practice and as a civic tool in schools and in democratic life beyond schools. In the Deweyan sense, media literacies have to be seen as central to the maintenance of a vibrant civil society. A democratizing education cannot exclude the teaching of media literacy. A core part of this work is also reclaiming the purpose and potential of post-industrial schooling. Certainly, schools will still exist as places that prepare the young for the world of work, but for most of their history, schools have also served other purposes. It is possible in the post-industrial era, then, that media production will become one of many new practices in schooling that exists for both a new and an old logic: civic education. Schools should be humanizing spaces and not just institutions that transmit literacy and numeracy. Through the act of production and creating narratives using the tools of new media, students can become more fully human, and they can develop the power to share their stories with the world. Similar to Henry Louis Gates's image of African Americans who write themselves into being through their narratives, youth can—through the production and distribution of counter-media texts—encode themselves into being through their construction of knowledge and their hopes of changing the world. None of these activities can be underestimated, and we argue that they should be central to the project of schooling.

References

Acuña, R. (1988). *Occupied America: A history of Chicanos*. New York: Harper and Row.

Alim, H. S. (2006). *Roc the mic right: The language of hip-hop culture*. New York: Routledge.

Alvermann, D. (2001). *Effective literacy instruction for adolescents*. Executive Summary and Paper Commissioned by the National Reading Conference. Chicago: National Reading Conference.

Anyon, J. (1981). Social class and school knowledge. *Curriculum Inquiry, 11*(1), 3–42.

Apple, M. (1990). *Ideology and curriculum*. New York: Routledge.

Banks, J. (1981). *Multi-ethnic education: Theory and practice*. Boston: Allyn & Bacon.

Barton, D., & Hamilton, M. (1998). *Local literacies: Reading and writing in one community*. New York: Routledge.

Barton, D., & Hamilton, M. (2000). Literacy practices. In D. Barton, M. Hamilton, & R. Ivanic (Eds.), *Situated literacies: Reading and writing in context* (pp. 1–16). New York: Routledge.

Beach, R., Campano, G., & Edmiston, B. (2010). *Literacy tools in the classroom: Teaching through critical inquiry, grades 5–12*. New York: Teachers College Press.

Benson, S. (Ed.). (2003). *The Hispanic American almanac: A reference work on Hispanics in the United States*. Detroit, MI: Gale.

Bigelow, B., & Peterson, B. (Eds.). (1998). *Rethinking Columbus: The next 500 years*. Milwaukee, WI: Rethinking Schools.

Bigelow, B., & Peterson, B. (Eds.) (2002). *Rethinking globalization: Teaching for justice in an unjust world*. Milwaukee, WI: Rethinking Schools.

Blume, H. (2011, December 11). New teacher contract could shut down school choice program. *Los Angeles Times*. Available at http://articles.latimes.com/2011/dec/11/local/la-me-school-choice-20111211

Brown, A. (1992). Design experiments: Theoretical and methodological challenges in creating complex interventions in classroom settings. *The Journal of the Learning Sciences, 2*(2), 141–178.

Casen, G. (1994). *History of El Sereno*. Los Angeles, CA: El Sereno Coordinating Council.

College Board. (2008). *Coming to our senses: Education and the American future*. New York: Author.

Cooper, R., & Huh, C. (2008). Improving academic possibilities of students of color during the middle school to high school transition. In J. K. Asamen, M. L. Ellis, & G. L. Berrry (Eds.), *The SAGE handbook of child development, multiculturalism, and media* (pp. 129–142). Thousand Oaks, CA: SAGE Publications.

Darling-Hammond, L. (2002). *Redesigning high schools, what matters and what works: 10 features of good small schools.* Stanford, CA: School Redesign Network at Stanford University.

Davis, M. (2006). *City of quartz: Excavating the future in Los Angeles.* New York: Verso.

Denzin, N. (1994). Evaluating qualitative research in the poststructural moment: The lessons James Joyce teaches us. *Qualitative Studies in Education, 7*(4), 295–308.

Dewey, J. (1900). *The school and society.* Chicago: The University of Chicago Press.

Dewey, J. (1902). *The child and the curriculum.* Chicago: The University of Chicago Press.

Dewey, J. (1916). *Democracy and education: An introduction to the philosophy of education.* New York: MacMillan.

Douglass, F. (1997). *Narrative of the life of Frederick Douglass: An American slave.* New York: Dell. (Original work published 1845.)

Duncan-Andrade, J., & Morrell, E. (2008). *The art of critical pedagogy: Possibilities for moving from theory to practice in urban schools.* New York: Peter Lang.

Ed Data. (2011). Fiscal, demographic, and performance data on California's K–12 schools. Available at http://www.ed-data.k12.ca.us

Fairclough, N. (1989). *Language and power.* Upper Saddle River, NJ: Pearson.

Felding, A., & Schoenback, R. (2003). *Building academic literacy: An anthology for reading apprenticeship.* San Francisco: Jossey-Bass.

Ferreira, E., & Ferreira, J. (1997). *Making sense of the media: A handbook of popular education techniques.* New York: Monthly Review Press.

Fine, M. (1991). *Framing dropouts: Notes on the politics of an urban public high school.* Albany: State University of New York Press.

Foucault, M. (1972). *The archaeology of knowledge.* New York: Routledge.

Freire, P. (1970). *Pedagogy of the oppressed.* New York: Continuum.

Freire, P. (1998). *The Paulo Freire reader.* New York: Continuum.

Freire, P. (2005). *Teachers as cultural workers: Letters to those who dare teach.* Boulder, CO: Westview.

Friedman, T. (2007). *The world is flat: A brief history of the 21st century.* New York: Picador.

Gee, J. (2003). *What video games have to teach us about learning and literacy?* New York: Palgrave-MacMillan.

Geertz, C. (1983). *Local knowledge: Further essays in interpretive anthropology.* New York: Basic Books.

Giroux, H. A. (1996). *Fugitive cultures: Race, violence, and youth.* New York: Routledge.

Giroux, H. A. (1998). *Channel surfing: Racism, the media and the destruction of today's youth.* New York: St. Martin's Press.

Gramsci, A. (1971). *Selections from the prison notebooks.* New York: International Publishers.

Gumperz, J. J., & Hymes, D. (1972). *Directions in sociolinguistics: The ethnography of communication.* New York: Holt, Rinehart, and Winston.

Gutierrez, K. (2008). Developing a sociocritical literacy in the third space. *Reading Research Quarterly, 43*(2), 148–164.

Heath, S. B. (1982). Protean shapes in literacy events: Ever-shifting oral and literate traditions. In D. Tannen (Ed.), *Spoken and written language: Exploring orality and literacy* (pp. 91–118). Norwood, NJ: Ablex.

Hill, M. L. (2009). *Beats, rhymes, and classroom life: Hip-hop pedagogy and the politics of identity.* New York: Teachers College Press.

Hobbs, R. (2007). *Reading the media in high school: Media literacy in high school English.* New York: Teachers College Press.

hooks, b. (1994). *Teaching to transgress: Education as the practice of freedom.* New York: Routledge.

Ito, M., et al. (2009). *Hanging out, messing around, and geeking out: Kids living and learning with new media.* Cambridge, MA: MIT Press.

Johnson, A. J. (1995). Life after death: Critical pedagogy in an urban classroom. *Harvard Educational Review, 65*(2), 213–230.

Kellner, D. (1995). *Media culture: Cultural studies, identity and politics between the modern and the postmodern.* New York: Routledge.

Kellner, D., & Kim, G. (2010). YouTube, critical pedagogy, and media activism: An articulation. *Review of Education, Pedagogy & Cultural Studies, 32*(1), 3–36.

Kellner, D., & Share, J. (2007). Critical media literacy is not an option. *Learning Inquiry, 1*(1), 59–69.

Kincheloe, J. L., & McLaren, P. L. (1998). Rethinking critical theory and qualitative research. In N. K. Denzin & Y. S. Lincoln (Eds.), *The landscape of qualitative research: Theories and issues* (pp. 260–299). Thousand Oaks, CA: SAGE Publications.

Kinloch, V. (2010). *Harlem on our minds: Place, race, and the literacies of urban youth.* New York: Teachers College Press.

Kist, W. (2005). *New literacies in action: Teaching and learning in multiple media.* New York: Teachers College Press.

Kozol, J. (1991). *Savage inequalities: Children in America's schools.* New York: HarperCollins.

Kress, G. (2003). *Literacy in the new media age.* New York: Routledge.

Ladson-Billings, G. J. (1994). *The dreamkeepers: Successful teachers of African-American children.* San Francisco: Jossey-Bass.

Ladson-Billings, G. J. (1995). Toward a theory of culturally relevant pedagogy. *American Education Research Journal, 32*(3), 465–491.

Lave, J. (1996). Teaching, as learning in practice. *Mind, Culture, and Activity, 3*(3), 149–164.

Lave, J., & Wenger, E. (1991). *Situated learning: Legitimate peripheral participation.* Cambridge, UK: Cambridge University Press.

Lee, C. D. (2007). *Culture, literacy, and learning: Taking bloom in the midst of a whirlwind.* New York: Teachers College Press.

Lievrouw, L. (2011). *Alternative and activist new media.* Malden, MA: Polity.

Maciel, D., & Ortiz, D. (Eds.). (1996). *Chicanas/Chicanos at the crossroads: Social, economic, and political change.* Tucson: University of Arizona Press.

McIntyre, A. (2000). Constructing meaning about violence, school, and community: Participatory action research with urban youth. *The Urban Review, 32*(2), 123–154.

McLaren, P. (2011). Radical negativity: Music education for social justice. *Action, Criticism, and Theory for Music Education, 10*(1), 131–147.

McLoughlin, S. (2009). *A pedagogy of the blues.* Rotterdam: Sense Publishers.

Mendoza-Grado, V., & Salvador, R. (2003). Are Chicanos the same as Mexicans? Available at http://www.mexica.net/chicano.php [The Chicano Latino Network (CLNET)].

Morrell, E. (2004). *Linking literacy and popular culture: Finding connections for lifelong learning.* Norwood, MA: Christopher Gordon.

Morrell, E. (2008). *Critical literacy and urban youth: Pedagogies of access, dissent, and liberation.* New York: Routledge.

Morrell, E., & Duncan-Andrade, J. (2002). Toward a critical classroom discourse: Promoting academic literacy through engaging hip hop culture with urban youth. *English Journal, 91*(6), 88–94.

Muñoz, C. (2007). *Youth, identity, power: The Chicano movement.* New York: Verso.

National Council for the Social Studies. (2009). *NCSS position statement on media literacy.* Silver Spring, MD: Author.

Nieto, S., & Bode, P. (2007). *Affirming diversity: The sociopolitical context of multicultural education.* Boston: Allyn & Bacon.

Oakes, J. (1985). *Keeping track: How schools structure inequality.* New Haven, CT: Yale University Press.

Oakes, J., & Rogers, J. (2006). *Learning power: Organizing for education and justice.* New York: Teachers College Press.

Olson, C. (2012). The Casta paintings of Latin America. Available at http://students.depaul.edu/~arubio1/HCI201/H4/H4MAIN.htm

Palinscar, A. S. (2005). Working theory into and out of design experiments. *Learning Disabilities Research & Practice, 20*(4), 218–220.

Perry, T. (2003). Freedom for literacy and literacy for freedom: The African-American philosophy of education. In T. Perry, A. Hilliard, & C. Steele (Eds.), *Young, gifted, and Black: Promoting high achievement among African-American students* (pp. 11–51). Boston: Beacon.

Rogers, J., & Morrell, E. (2011). A force to reckon with: The Campaign for College Access in Los Angeles. In M. Orr & J. Rogers (Eds.), *Public engagement and public education: Joining forces to revitalize democracy and equalize schools* (pp. 227–250). Stanford, CA: Stanford University Press.

Rogoff, B. (1990). *Apprenticeship in thinking: Cognitive development in social context.* New York: Oxford.

Rose, T. (1994). *Black noise: Rap music and black culture in contemporary America.* Middletown, CT: Wesleyan Press.

Scholes, R. (1999). *The rise and fall of English: Reconstructing English as a discipline.* New Haven, CT: Yale University Press.

Selman, R. (2003). *The promotion of social awareness: Powerful lessons from the partnership of developmental theory and classroom practice.* New York: Russell Sage Foundation.

Sitomer, A., & Cirelli, M. (2004). *Hip-hop poetry and the classics: Connecting our classic curriculum to hip-hop poetry through standards-based language arts instruction.* Beverly Hills, CA: Milk Mug Publishing.

Spivak, G. (1988). Can the subaltern speak? In C. Nelson & L. Grossberg (Eds.), *Marxism and the interpretations of culture* (pp. 271–313). London: Macmillan.

Steele, C., & Aronson, J. (1995). Stereotype threat and the intellectual test performance of African-Americans. *Journal of Personality and Social Psychology, 69*(5), 797–811.

Steinberg, S., & Kincheloe, J. (2004). *Kinderculture: The corporate construction of childhood.* Boulder, CO: Westview Press.

Street, B. (1984). *Literacy in theory and practice.* Cambridge, UK: Cambridge University Press.

Thoman, E., & Jolls, T. (2003). *Media literacy: A national priority for a changing world.* Available at http://www.medialit.org/reading-room/media-literacy-national-priority-changing-world

U.S. Department of Education. (2010). *The blueprint for educational reform.* Washington, DC: Author.

Valenzuela, A. (1999). *Subtractive schooling: U.S.-Mexican youth and the politics of caring.* Albany: State University of New York Press.

Villa, R., & Sanchez, G. (2005). *Los Angeles and the future of urban cultures.* Baltimore: The John Hopkins University Press.

Wenger, E. (1998). *Communities of practice: Learning, meaning, and identity.* New York: Cambridge University Press.

Williams, R. (1958). *Culture and society.* London: Chatto and Windus.

Williams, S. (2006). *The dead emcee scrolls: The lost teachings of hip hop.* New York: MTV Books.

Winn, M., & Behizadeh, N. (2011). The right to be literate: Literacy, education, and the school-to-prison pipeline. *Review of Research in Education, 35*(1), 147–173.

Woodson, C. G. (1972). *Miseducation of the Negro.* New York: AMS Press.

Yosso, T. J. (2005). Whose culture has capital? A critical race theory discussion of community cultural wealth. *Race Ethnicity and Education, 8*(1), 69–91.

Zollers, A. (2009). Critical perspectives on social network sites. In R. Hammer & D. Kellner (Eds.), *Media cultural studies: Critical approaches* (pp. 602–614). New York: Peter Lang.

Index

About the Authors

Ernest Morrell is a professor of English Education and director of the Institute for Urban and Minority Education (IUME) at Teachers College, Columbia University. He has interests in youth popular culture, literacy education, participatory action research, teacher development, and the transformation of city schools. Morrell received his doctorate from the University of California–Berkeley and began his career teaching and coaching in Oakland Public Schools.

Rudy Dueñas is a teacher of social studies in the Agents of Change Small Learning Community at Wilson High School in Los Angeles. He has interests in ethnic studies, youth participatory action video making, and youth empowerment. Dueñas helped develop a network of student clubs called The Urban Visionaries, which encourage youth to become change agents in their communities using conscious hip hop (Hip-Hop Club), culture (MEChA), cycling (Crank Heads), and food justice (TREE Club).

Veronica Garcia is a former English teacher at Wilson High School in Los Angeles and currently an education doctoral candidate at the University of Southern California. Her dissertation focuses on the literacy experiences of formerly incarcerated young Latino males. Her interests also include teacher preparation, critical literacy and curriculum development, student action research, juvenile justice education, and student voice.

Jorge López is a teacher of social studies at the school of Communications, New Media, and Technology at Roosevelt High School in Los Angeles. He has interests in youth organizing, urban art education, ethnic studies, critical literacy, and community empowerment. López continues to serve the Boyle Heights neighborhood through community partnerships and projects.